God Meant It for Good

The Life of Joseph
Volume 2

Genesis 42-50

DR. DAVID JEREMIAH

with Dr. David Jeremiah

© 1996 by Turning Point for God
P.O. Box 3838
San Diego, CA 92163
All Rights Reserved

Published by Walk Thru the Bible Ministries, Atlanta, Georgia.

Unless otherwise indicated, Scripture verses quoted are taken from the NEW KING JAMES VERSION.

Printed in the United States of America.

Contents

About Dr. David Jeremiah and Turning Point

Dr. David Jeremiah is the founder of Turning Point, a ministry committed to providing Christians with sound Bible teaching relevant to today's changing times through radio broadcasts, audiocassette series, and books. Dr. Jeremiah's "common sense" teaching on topics such as family, stress, the New Age, angels, and biblical prophecy forms the foundation of Turning Point.

Dr. Jeremiah is the senior pastor of Shadow Mountain Community Church in El Cajon near San Diego, California, where he also serves as president of Christian Heritage College. He and his wife, Donna, have four children.

In 1982, Dr. Jeremiah brought the same solid teaching to San Diego television that he shares weekly with his congregation. Shortly thereafter, Turning Point expanded its ministry to radio. Dr. Jeremiah's inspiring messages are currently broadcast weekly from more than 300 national and international radio stations.

Because Dr. Jeremiah desires to know his listening audience, he travels nationwide holding "A Night of Encouragement" radio rallies and Spiritual Enrichment conferences that touch the hearts and lives of many. According to Dr. Jeremiah, "At some point in time, everyone reaches a turning point, and for every person that moment is unique, an experience to hold onto forever. There's so much changing in today's world that sometimes it's difficult to always choose the right path. Turning Point offers people an understanding of God's Word, as well as the opportunity to make a difference in their lives."

Dr. Jeremiah has authored ten books including *Escape the Coming Night* (Revelation), *The Handwriting on the Wall* (Daniel), *Turning Toward Joy* (Philippians), *Turning Toward Integrity* (James), *The Power of Encouragement*, *Invasion of Other Gods* (New Age), *Overcoming Loneliness*, and his latest release, *What the Bible Says About Angels*.

About This Study Guide

T he purpose of this Turning Point study guide is to reinforce Dr. David Jeremiah's dynamic, in-depth teaching on the life of Joseph and to aid the reader in applying biblical truth to his or her daily life. This study guide is designed to be used in conjunction with Dr. Jeremiah's *God Meant It for Good* audiocassette series on the life of Joseph, but it may also be used by itself for personal or group Bible study.

Structure of the Lessons

Each lesson is based on one of the tapes in the *God Meant It for Good* audiocassette series and focuses on passages in the Bible. Each lesson is composed of the following elements:

• Outline

The outline at the beginning of the lesson gives a clear, concise picture of the topic being studied and provides a helpful framework for readers as they listen to Dr. Jeremiah's teaching.

• Overview

The overview summarizes Dr. Jeremiah's teaching on the topic being studied in the lesson. Readers should refer to their own Bibles as they study the overview.

• Application

This section contains a variety of questions designed to help readers dig deeper into the lesson and the Scriptures and to apply the lesson to their daily lives. For Bible study groups or Sunday school classes, these questions will provide a springboard for group discussion and interaction.

• Did You Know?

This section presents a fun fact, historical note, or insight which adds a point of interest to the preceding lesson.

Using This Guide for Group Study

The lessons in this study guide are suitable for Sunday school classes, small group studies, elective Bible studies, or home Bible study groups. Each person in the group should have his or her own study guide.

When possible, the study guide should be used with the corresponding tape series. You may wish to assign the study guide as homework prior to the meeting and then use the meeting time to listen to the tape and discuss the lesson.

For Continuing Study

A complete catalog of Dr. Jeremiah's materials for personal and group study is available through Turning Point. To obtain a catalog, additional study guides, or more information about Turning Point, call 1-800-947-1993 or write to: Turning Point, P.O. Box 3838, San Diego, CA 92163.

Dr. Jeremiah's "Turning Point" radio broadcast is currently heard on more than 300 national and international radio stations. Contact your local Christian radio station or Turning Point for program times in your area.

God Meant It for Good

The Life of Joseph • Volume 2

INTRODUCTION

I once heard a speaker, the youngest son of a poor Dutch immigrant, tell of the hardships his family endured at the hands of others. His father passed away at a young age, leaving his mother with five young mouths to feed, in a country where she struggled with the language and the customs. The neighbor ladies were cruel, acting haughty toward them and constantly criticizing his mother, tearing her down for her accent, her poverty, and her leaving five children in order to earn enough money to live. The man explained that one day his mother snapped. This normally quiet woman stormed across the street in a rage, lit into the neighbor, and offered a frenzied defense of her beloved brood of kids. Then she came back across the street and threw up, spending the rest of the evening weeping in the bathroom.

There are times I can identify with that harried mother, for I've had a few experiences like that of my own. When it gets to the point where you just can't take it any more, it's like the valve pops open. You march across the street, or into the boss's office, or over to the church, and you just let it all out. The vengeance flows. But as good as that might have seemed for the moment, it probably wasn't right. Taking revenge rarely leads to a positive outcome.

The life of Joseph is probably the antithesis to that sort of activity, for if there was ever a man who had reason to take revenge, it was Joseph. His family had badly mistreated him for a dream that turned out to be precisely correct. Their actions had led to years of slavery, unjust accusations, and the hardships of prison. He had every right to get back at his brothers . . . but he didn't.

In a golf book I read recently, the author told a story about making a nearly impossible shot around a tree by hitting the ball high and letting the strong wind carry it toward the green. A good golfer makes use of the wind, rather than fighting it. He learns to allow the wind to push his ball where it will, instead of trying to battle and control what he cannot. As it is in golf, so it is in life. Our lives are often battered by storms that attack our confidence, our resources, and our plans. But as Christians, we can understand that God is in all those gales. He is there with us, using the storms to shape our character. We can either become bitter because of the winds of life, or we can allow them to make us better, stronger people.

If ever a man had reason to be bitter, it was Joseph. His family had badly mistreated him for a dream that in fact turned out to be precisely correct. Their actions led to Joseph's years of slavery, to unjust accusations, even to the hardships of prison. He had every right to get back at his brothers . . . but he didn't.

Instead, Joseph made use of the stormy winds that battered his life, always focusing on God's purpose for his life. As we study his life, we learn how he was able to recognize that God was shaping him for an important mission—that of providing a safe haven for his family.

In this study of the second part of Joseph's life, you will explore the challenging issues of betrayal, disappointment, forgiveness, and the eventual reconciliation of Joseph with his brothers, as well as his provision for them of a new homeland in this dire time of drought. There are many liberating truths which we can learn from the way Joseph faced these obstacles. We, too, experience difficult times, and God uses each one as an opportunity to teach us valuable lessons so that we can be ready to accomplish His will.

GOD'S METHOD FOR MELTING HARD HEARTS

Genesis 42:1-24

*In this lesson we will take a look at Joseph's brothers
and Jacob's decision to send them to Egypt.*

OUTLINE

The Lord has a way of melting even the hardest hearts. In this
chapter, He arranges circumstances so that Joseph's brothers
face their actions and the consequences of their sin.

I. **The Experience of Difficulty**
II. **The Exclusion of Trust**
   A. Why Didn't They Recognize Joseph?
III. **The Exile in Prison**
IV. **The Exposure of the Heart**
V. **The Expression of Kindness**

T he last twenty years in the life of Jacob's family had settled into a routine. Still living in Canaan, Jacob and his eleven sons carried on their shepherding trade and continued interacting with the Canaanites. Once in a while, Jacob would cry when he thought of Joseph, his teenage son who disappeared mysteriously while checking on his brothers in Dothan, but time had passed and some of the sting of his loss was gone. Jacob still had Benjamin, his other son by Rachel, and the boy had turned into a fine young man. The other ten boys had almost been able to bury their memories of Joseph, though sometimes the evil they had done would come to mind. But with the passing of twenty years, they had erased most of the awful details and settled into a forgetfulness born of time.

But twenty years is not too long for God to remember, and what is about to unfold is one of the most amazing scenarios of God's dealing with long-past sin. For, while Joseph was being dealt with by God in Egypt, the Lord was also setting the stage for the recovery of Joseph's family. They were His chosen people, and no pain would be spared in bringing the family and Joseph back together. Even a world-wide famine could be employed to bring a small tribe of seventy souls to Egypt where they could grow into a large nation unaffected by evil neighbors. Of course, more important than getting the family back to Joseph was getting the family back to God. The Lord had to melt their hard hearts and bring to full realization the guilt and sin of their evil treatment of Joseph. In Genesis 42 we see the Lord's methods for bringing about change in people. He still uses those methods, still works according to the principles of His divine sovereignty to bring His children in line with His will. If you have ever been far outside His will, you will no doubt see yourself in this chapter, remember how God dealt with you, and marvel at the grace and love of your Heavenly Father. There are a number of steps the Lord takes to melt the hardened hearts of Jacob's sons and bring them first to conviction and, ultimately, to fellowship with Him.

The Experience of Difficulty

Often, when we are away from the Lord, He brings difficulty into our lives to get our attention. In the first few verses of chapter 42, the Lord brought hunger to the family of Jacob: "When Jacob saw that there was grain in Egypt, Jacob said to his sons, 'Why do you look at one another?' And he said, 'Indeed I have heard that there is grain in Egypt; go down to that place and buy for us there, that we may live and not die.' So Joseph's ten brothers went down to buy grain in Egypt" (Genesis 42:1-3).

Joseph had prophesied the famine when he interpreted Pharaoh's dream, and twice in the text we are told it was a severe famine, extending to the entire known world. When the grain was gone and the food running low, the father realized something had to be done. He looked at his sons, who were apparently indecisive about what to do, and said, "Don't just sit there looking at each other."

I find it interesting that what initially moved them toward repentance was a problem. Nearly every miracle in the New Testament is the result of a problem, and many of the miracles in our lives come as a result of our responding to the problems God sends our way. Of course, not every problem is God's method of bringing us to repentance, since every Christian can expect difficulties as part of the growth process. But the Lord often uses problems to get the attention of His wayward children. Most of us can probably point to a time in our lives when we began to stray from the Lord, and the Lord brought us back through some problem in our lives. That's often His first step.

The Exclusion of Trust

"But Jacob did not send Joseph's brother Benjamin with his brothers, for he said, 'Lest some calamity befall him'" (v. 4). We'll see how important Benjamin was to his father a bit later in the chapter, but this verse offers a hint of the distrust Jacob harbored in his heart toward the other ten boys. Twenty years could not have gone by without there having been some incident between them that caused doubt in Jacob's mind concerning his beloved son Joseph. Sometimes, when he looked at his sons, Jacob saw guilt on their faces. So the father didn't trust his boys to take Benjamin with them to buy grain, for he had never completely reconciled in his mind their story of Joseph's blood-stained coat. Somehow it didn't add up, and as the years had gone by, Jacob had developed some mistrust toward the boys, which they noticed. His sons were no longer young, and they must have known of their father's suspicions. Insecurity is the product of being out of God's will.

And the sons of Israel went to buy grain among those
who journeyed, for the famine was in the land of
Canaan. Now Joseph was governor over the land; and
it was he who sold to all the people of the land. And
Joseph's brothers came and bowed down before him
with their faces to the earth. Joseph saw his brothers
and recognized them, but he acted as a stranger to
them and spoke roughly to them. Then he said to
them, "Where do you come from?" And they said,
"From the land of Canaan to buy food." So Joseph
recognized his brothers, but they did not recognize
him. Then Joseph remembered the dreams which he
had dreamed about them, and said to them, "You are
spies! You have come to see the nakedness of the
land!" And they said to him, "No, my lord, but your
servants have come to buy food. We are all one man's
sons; we are honest men; your servants are not spies."
But he said to them, "No, but you have come to see
the nakedness of the land." And they said, "Your servants are twelve brothers, the sons of one man in the
land of Canaan; and in fact, the youngest is with our
father today, and one is no more." But Joseph said to
them, "It is as I spoke to you, saying, 'You are spies.'
In this manner you shall be tested: By the life of
Pharaoh, you shall not leave this place unless your
youngest brother comes here" (Genesis 42:5-15).

What is happening is the gradual unfolding of their own sin. God
designs an amazing episode in the lives of these men. As they come
to Egypt with their father's mandate to buy grain, they are ushered
through the crowded streets to a special place where grain is dis-
pensed to non-Egyptians. Joseph, who is in charge of all the land
and food distribution, took special care to personally dispense grain
to those outside of Egypt. So those boys stand before the very
brother whom they sold into slavery twenty years earlier. They bow
down before him, just as Joseph had dreamed they would.

Why Didn't They Recognize Joseph?
Some have been troubled that, out of the ten brothers, not one
recognized Joseph. There are a number of factors contributing to
their failure to recognize him. The first is his appearance. Joseph

was clean-shaven, with a shaved head, long robe, and different clothes. He appeared as an Egyptian, not a Hebrew. A second factor is that of age. The last time they saw Joseph, he was a lad of seventeen. Now he was a grown man, almost forty, with the usual physical changes that every man goes through. Also, when Joseph spoke to his brothers, he did so in Egyptian, using an interpreter. He didn't appear to understand their language, which would also have contributed to their failure to recognize him. In addition, his authority would have surprised them. The last they knew, Joseph was on a camel train as a slave. Who would have thought that in a short period of time their brother would rise from slave to the second most powerful position in all of Egypt? They never expected to see Joseph in such a position.

Finally, the Scriptures tell us that Joseph was involved in a bit of acting. The original language tells us that Joseph "made himself unrecognizable" to his brothers. He play-acted. He spoke roughly to them and was not willing to have them recognize him yet. Why did he disguise himself? Why keep his identity from them and hold off a grand reunion? There are many possible explanations. Some have suggested that Joseph used rough treatment in order to keep his own emotions under control. Perhaps he hid behind a gruff exterior to keep his heart from breaking at the sight of his own flesh and blood appearing before him. Others have proposed that Joseph was acting by inspiration, remembering his dreams about his brothers bowing before him. Perhaps the Lord restrained Joseph from revealing himself to his family. Still others have put forth the idea that Joseph simply wanted to subject his brothers to the same opportunity to grow as he had, so he put them through a bitter experience to purge them from their wickedness.

As I've studied the passage, I think the reason Joseph disguised himself was to repeat for his brothers the last experience they had together. Joseph had been sent to check up on his brothers, and his brothers accused him of "spying" on them for Jacob. So Joseph watched his brothers come kneel down before him, and in the providence of God he accuses them of being spies. They had thrown him into a pit, so he throws them into jail. Sometimes when we are victims of the same treatment we have given to others, God allows it to create in us a sensitivity to our own sin. Little by little the brothers have a growing consciousness of their own sin. When they first came, they had basically forgotten their actions toward Joseph. But being accused of spying causes them to remember they had another brother, one who is with them no more. Their evil actions toward Joseph crept into the back of their minds.

The Exile In Prison

"Send one of you, and let him bring your brother; and you shall be kept in prison, that your words may be tested to see whether there is any truth in you; or else, by the life of Pharaoh, surely you are spies!" So he put them all together in prison three days. Then Joseph said to them the third day, "Do this and live, for I fear God: If you are honest men, let one of your brothers be confined to your prison house; but you, go and carry grain for the famine of your houses. And bring your youngest brother to me; so your words will be verified, and you shall not die." And they did so (vv. 16-20).

God used solitary confinement to break the hearts of those men. They are away from home, walking through a strange land and listening to a language they do not understand when Joseph accuses them of being spies and isolates them in the very prison house where he languished for more than two long years.

It's not hard to imagine the conversations that took place in that prison. Those men must have talked through everything they had done. Their treatment of Joseph was now in the forefront of their minds as they considered their situation. On the third day, when Joseph brought them all out of prison, he offered them a chance for redemption. Rather than insisting they all stay, he will make only one brother stay, while the rest go back and get Benjamin. Joseph must have been on the verge of breaking. His compassion and his love for God are evident, but he doesn't yet know if he can trust his brothers.

The Exposure of the Heart

Then they said to one another, "We are truly guilty concerning our brother, for we saw the anguish of his soul when he pleaded with us, and we would not hear; therefore this distress has come upon us." And Reuben answered them, saying, "Did I not speak to you, saying, 'Do not sin against the boy'; and you would not listen? Therefore behold, his blood is now required of us." But they did not know that Joseph understood them, for he spoke to them through an interpreter. And he turned himself away from them and wept. Then he returned to them again, and talked with them. And he took Simeon from them and bound him before their eyes (vv. 21-24).

As their conviction grew, the boys began to review their sin. The one they held in common came to their memory like a ghost out of a dark night. As they talked about it, their sin came back too vividly: their innocent young brother struggling and screaming in a pit; his voice wailing for help as they sit down to eat a meal; tears streaming down his face as they sell him to the Ishmaelites. "We are guilty," they said to themselves, "and we're getting what we deserve." Their hearts were exposed as wicked.

Joseph couldn't hold out any longer. Hearing his brothers describe their actions of so many years ago, he rushes away and explodes in emotion and tears. When he finally gets control of himself and comes back, he chooses Simeon to be bound while the others are sent back to Canaan. Simeon was often the ring-leader involved in the bad things that went on in the family, and he failed to come to Joseph's aid as the second-oldest son. He couldn't have been a very good fellow—on his deathbed, Jacob had nothing good to say about Simeon. So he was kept in prison while the others went back to their father.

The Expression of Kindness

Then Joseph gave a command to fill their sacks with grain, to restore every man's money to his sack, and to give them provisions for the journey. Thus he did for them. So they loaded their donkeys with the grain and departed from there. But as one of them opened his sack to give his donkey feed at the encampment, he saw his money; and there it was, in the mouth of his sack. So he said to his brothers, "My money has been restored, and there it is, in my sack!" Then their hearts failed them and they were afraid, saying to one another, "What is this that God has done to us?" (vv. 25-28).

As recipients of undeserved grace, God brings us to a position of conviction for our sin. The brothers wouldn't have been afraid if they had done nothing wrong. But their lives had been filled with sin, so they were afraid.

Joseph, on the other hand, acted from a pure heart. He couldn't bring himself to charge his brothers for grain that was needed by his family back in Canaan. So as an act of kindness, he restored to every man's sack the money he had paid. But those boys who had sold their brother for twenty shekels loathed the money. They saw it as blood money and wanted to get rid of it, for it spoke of their sin. When they got home, they must have told Jacob everything that happened, except for the sin they all carried with them.

This part of the story reveals the difference between *regret* and *repentance*. Joseph's brothers regretted what they had done but had not yet repented of their sin. They no longer wanted to live with the consequences of their actions, but they refused to turn to God for forgiveness. Each of us must not only regret our mistakes but go before the Lord and repent of our willful sin. Only then will we find the forgiveness and grace the Lord offers. And He will remember our sins no more, for *forgiveness—forgets*.

APPLICATION

---

1. Why is an experience of difficulty sometimes necessary for us to change?

In your view, what causes a person to harden his or her heart?

When have you wandered away from the Lord?

What brought you back?

2. Why didn't Jacob trust his boys?

Tell about a time when someone broke trust with you. How did you feel?

How is trust regained?

3. Why didn't Joseph reveal himself to his brothers immediately?

Did he accuse them of being spies to "get back" at them?

How did their time in prison change them?

4. Is there anything in your life that is keeping you away from God right now?

What is it?

What do you need to do to make things right between you and the Lord?

5. How did Peter break the trust of Jesus in Matthew 26:31-35 and 69-75?

How did the Lord melt the heart of Peter in John 21:15-19?

What did the Lord use to melt the hard heart of Paul in Acts 8:1-3 and 9:1-30?

6.   What is the difference between regret and repentance?

Can you think of a biblical example of each?

What does "forgetting" have to do with "forgiveness"?

Does God forget as well as forgive?

What would you say to a person who told you, "I can forgive, but I'll never forget!"?

7. Spend a few moments in prayer, focusing on all the Lord has forgiven you. Make sure to examine your life to see if there is an area in which you have become hard-hearted.

DID YOU KNOW?

The journey from Hebron, where Jacob's family lived, to the Egyptian city of On was more than 350 miles. For Joseph's brothers to come such a long way in search of food means the drought must have been extremely bad. The journey meant crossing the mountains and the Negev desert, so the journey must have taken more than two weeks each way!

Lesson 2

FROM FAMINE TO FEAST

Genesis 42:25-43:34

*This chapter will explore Joseph's dealings with
his brothers in Egypt.*

OUTLINE

When Joseph's brothers returned to their father with grain, they faced a difficult problem: When do they go back to get Simeon, and how will they get their father to agree to allow them to return with Benjamin? Chapter 43 reveals their struggle in deciding how to tackle the problem.

   I. The Shortage that Demands the Promise
  II. The Sense that Determines the Promise
 III. The Sincerity that Declares the Promise
  IV. The Success that Develops the Promise
   V. Lessons from the Story

I f you've spent much time in airports, you know the emotions that are common among those in the terminal. Some people are crying as they say good-bye to loved ones. Others are rejoicing, offering big hugs to long-lost friends. Joseph and his brothers felt the same sorts of emotions. God used the process of gradual re-acquaintance to break down the hard hearts of those ten brothers and to bring them back to Himself.

When the boys returned to their father, they told him all about the strange Egyptian ruler who asked about their father and kept their brother prisoner. They had the grain they'd bought, but they also found the money they had paid. The boys had made some spiritual progress, for they told their father the truth rather than resorting to some foolish story as they had upon the disappearance of Joseph. They didn't try to cover up the Egyptian's desire to see their youngest brother, Benjamin. But Jacob was unwilling to allow Benjamin to return with them. He had already lost Joseph, then Simeon, and he was unwilling to part with Benjamin, the last evidence of his relationship with his beloved Rachel. Reuben, the oldest boy, offered his own sons as a pledge, but Jacob wasn't interested in making any deals. He wanted to protect his youngest boy.

What happened next is interesting. Leadership in the family seems to turn from Reuben to Judah. He makes a promise to his father that sets in motion the return of Joseph to their family.

The Shortage that Demands the Promise

"Now the famine was severe in the land. And it came to pass, when they had eaten up the grain which they had brought from Egypt, that their father said to them, 'Go back, buy us a little food'" (Genesis 43:1-2). This was the motivation God used to get the brothers to Egypt in the first place, but the Lord had not yet accomplished His entire plan for them, so he again drives them back to a waiting Joseph. Their grain has run out, and there is a severe famine in the land. Their shortage meant a return to Egypt, but it would demand a promise of protection for Benjamin.

The Sense that Determines the Promise

Judah told Jacob that Joseph solemnly warned them not to

return to Egypt without Benjamin. So, if Jacob would send Benjamin with them, they would go down and buy food . . . "But if you will not send him, we will not go down; for the man said to us, 'You shall not see my face unless your brother is with you'" (vv. 4-5). Judah reminded his father of the stipulations made for their purchase of grain, but it only seemed to anger his father, who accused the boys of bargaining with Benjamin's life. So Judah made a very sensible promise to his father: "Send the lad with me, and we will arise and go, that we may live and not die, both we and you and also our little ones. I myself will be surety for him; from my hand you shall require him. If I do not bring him back to you and set him before you, then let me bear the blame forever" (vv. 8-9).

Judah logically relates what must happen to keep the family from starving. What he says makes sense. Jacob didn't want to send Benjamin, but without him there would be no food.

The Sincerity that Declares the Promise

Judah promises his father, "I'll be responsible for little Ben." He even puts his own life on the line, promising that he would take full responsibility if anything were to happen to Benjamin. Then Judah argues, "For if we had not lingered, surely by now we would have returned this second time" (v. 10).

I think Judah had grown up quite a bit in those twenty years Joseph was gone. Whereas Reuben was willing to give up his sons, Judah was willing to give his own life. He promised to take personal responsibility for Benjamin. He also began to be the spokesman for his brothers, so perhaps he had outgrown that rebellious streak he'd had as a young man. His sincerity convinced his father to let them go: "And their father Israel said to them, 'If it must be so . . . '" (v. 11).

The Success that Develops the Promise

The logic of Judah's argument won their father over. He encouraged them to go and to take gifts of fruit and nuts and spices and double the money required, so they could pay for their last trip, if someone asked. Jacob realized there was no other option. It's amazing how God arranged all the circumstances to move that family in the direction He wanted them to go. There was no sense arguing about Benjamin's protection if he was going to starve to death at home. So the boys took along everything that hadn't been touched by the famine: dried fruit, balm, honey, and myrrh. "The men took that present and Benjamin, and they took double money in their hand, and arose and went down to Egypt; and they stood before Joseph" (v. 15).

This time the ten brothers have Benjamin with them, and they re-tell the story of finding their money in their knapsacks,

> And when Joseph came home, they brought him the present which was in their hand into the house, and bowed down before him to the earth. Then he asked them about their well-being, and said, "Is your father well, the old man of whom you spoke? Is he still alive?" And they answered, "Your servant our father is in good health; he is still alive." And they bowed their heads down and prostrated themselves (vv. 26-28).

When I think of those months Joseph waited, my heart aches for him. His father might have died in the meantime, and he wasn't sure how soon the brothers would return to get Simeon, so Joseph must have suffered in keeping his secret inside. But when he looked up and saw Benjamin, Joseph could hold it no longer. "Now his heart yearned for his brother; so Joseph made haste and sought somewhere to weep. And he went into his chamber and wept there. Then he washed his face and came out; and he restrained himself, and said, 'Serve the bread'" (vv. 30-31).

Joseph's brothers had to be moved by the fear of God, but Joseph himself was moved by the love of God. A man or woman who is not broken-hearted over sin may still be moved by the display of love God reveals in sending Jesus to die on the cross. When we fall into sin, we need to remember that our sin nailed our blessed Savior to the cross, and we need to weep both for our sin and over God's love. Joseph, like Christ, continued to love his brothers, though they had wronged him. The Lord Jesus loves us though our sin nailed Him to that tree. God sometimes breaks hard hearts through love.

He also breaks them through knowledge, and Joseph reveals to his brothers that he has a special knowledge about them. As Joseph walked in, the table was spread with food, and he proceeded to give the correct seating order. The Bible says that Joseph "astonished" his brothers by seating them according to their birthdays and by giving Benjamin the greatest portions, showing to them that he recognized Benjamin's importance in the family. Joseph is gradually revealing himself to his brothers, but they are mystified by his knowledge. Again, there is something wonderful in how Joseph acts toward his brothers. He knew them and was ready to reveal his knowledge about them. God knows us; He knows more about us than anyone else. One day we'll have to give an account to Him for our lives. Everything will be open before Him. If that doesn't give us pause to think, nothing will.

There is evidence in this chapter that God's work was starting to make a difference in the lives of the brothers. After the waiters had served all the other men, Benjamin was served five times as much, yet none of the others complained. I believe Joseph ordered the waiters to do that so he could see if the others still had a problem with jealousy. Nobody leaped up to ask, "How come he got five times as much as me?" There is not one word of complaint recorded. The brothers were starting to understand how their attitudes had affected their decisions. God had begun to penetrate their hearts. As a matter of fact, verse 34 notes that "they drank and were merry" with Joseph, so while they still didn't know who he was, at least they were appreciative of what he had done.

Lessons from the Story

As I look over Genesis 43, I am reminded of the place of fear in the program of God. When I was growing up, we used to read all the verses in Proverbs that warn us that "the fear of the Lord is the beginning of wisdom." The Scripture calls us to fear God, but my teachers would always try to explain those words away. I remember being told that the word *fear* was a reference to respect or awe, not to actually being afraid of God. As a pastor, I'm not so sure. There is scarcely anything more striking in this story than the fear Joseph's brethren had. On their first journey, they were fearful of what they might find. On their way home, they were fearful when they found money in their sacks. Fear continued to affect them as they returned to meet Joseph. And once they head for home, they will experience an even greater fear when Benjamin is arrested!

God often uses fear to call the heart to repent. Fear warns, searches, and purifies the believer. It has a tendency to keep our hearts tender, to make us shrink from sin, and to cause us to be sensitive to God's will. Fear helps us be true to the Lord, and we might as well admit it. I know of very few subjects in the Word of God which are more worthy of in-depth study than the fear of God. In our culture we have tried to bring God down to man's level, and in doing so, we have done away with our fear of a holy God.

As you read the life of Joseph, learn *the place of fear in the program of God*. There is a righteous fear that ought to fill the heart of every believer. Just as Joseph's brothers trembled in fear as they considered the great power Joseph had over them, we ought to tremble in knowing that the great God of the universe has all power over every circumstance in our lives.

A second impression I get as I look back over this story is *the priority of repentance in the program of God*. The Lord wanted these boys to repent. He expected them to be sorrowful, to make amends, and to change the direction of their lives. God was not going to be satisfied with a shallow repentance that would keep these guys from having to face the consequences; He wanted a genuine repentance evidenced by a changed life. Some people will repent just enough to take the pressure off or so they'll feel better about themselves. But repentance is a way of saying, "God, I know I've done wrong, and I'm sorry. Please forgive me, and help me to go in a new direction."

The reason the Lord took so long in working out His program in the lives of Joseph's brothers was that He wanted to test them over time, to see if their repentance was real. It was necessary for Joseph to see the reality of their changed lives, so the long gaps between the first and second meetings with his brothers were orchestrated by God. We need to recall the importance of repentance. It's too easy to encourage people to "just believe," and I believe faith is the only requirement for salvation. But, if you have faith in God, you also have repentance from sin. When you turn toward God, you turn away from sin. True repentance means to change your direction, to change your mind.

A third impression I get as I read this story is *the possibility of recovery in the program of God*. Consider Joseph's brother Judah. When he was born, Judah's mother was so excited she began to sing praises to God. She even named him Judah, which means praise. But as you watch this little tyke grow up, you start to wonder what happened to the praise! As a young man, Judah was the one who suggested they sell Joseph rather than simply kill him. Later, he grew up and married a pagan, broke promises to people, and committed incest with his daughter-in-law. But in this story, something starts to happen to Judah. Perhaps it is the pressure of poverty, or his deepening love for his family, or maybe his own self-confidence has simply been so shaken through all that's happened, that Judah decides to step forward and become a leader. He moves from being a man living for himself to a man living for God. On his father's deathbed, Judah was praised as being a "lion" and the one his brothers looked up to. It was through Judah that Jesus Christ's lineage came.

That tells us it is never too late to change. It's never too late for God to change our lives. He wants to bring wayward people back to Himself. There is always the possibility of recovery in the program of God. The Lord has done all He can to mark the way back, and at some point in time the evil Judah decided to head in that direction. "It's time to live right," he said to himself. "It's time to be praise for Jehovah." God is still in the business of changing lives. He is still calling people to repent and come back to Him. There is always the possibility of recovery in the program of God.

APPLICATION

1. In Genesis chapter 43, what promise did Judah make to his father?

What shortage prompted that promise?

Why is it significant that Judah made that promise?

2. How did Joseph treat his brothers?

Why was Benjamin offered special treatment?

What evidence is there that the brothers were starting to change?

3. List the big turning points in your spiritual life.

Why were they so significant?

4. What was your life like before you met Christ?

How did you meet the Lord?

In what ways has your life changed since meeting Him?

5.   Read Proverbs chapter 1. What does it mean to "fear" the Lord?

How could being afraid of a holy God be a good thing?

How would you respond to someone who said to you, "Oh, we don't need to fear God. God is our friend. The old concept of a fearful, terrible God just won't be accepted any more"?

6. What principles for repentance can you glean from the following passages?

   Isaiah 30:15

   Jeremiah 5:1-4

   Luke 3:3-14

   Luke 5:32

   Acts 17:29-31

   Acts 26:20

   Romans 2:2-5

   2 Corinthians 7:8-11

   2 Peter 3:9

7. What happened in Judah's life in Genesis 38?

What would you say to someone complaining that it is "too late" for them to come to Christ?

Write a poem or a psalm to the Lord, praising Him for His forgiveness and for arranging the circumstances of our lives.

DID YOU KNOW?

The word *repent* was actually a cartographer's term. It meant "to change direction," and was commonly used with those driving caravans in the open spaces of Palestine. When we repent, we change direction in our lives. Rather than moving away from God, we begin moving toward Him.

Lesson 3

JOSEPH'S CONSPIRACY

Genesis 44:1-34

This chapter will examine Joseph's actions in drawing his family toward Egypt.

OUTLINE

J ust as God tested Joseph and prepared him to serve, now the Lord uses Joseph as His instrument in testing Joseph's family. The tremendous deliberation with which God dealt with Joseph will now be put into practice in his brothers' lives, in order to bring them to repentance and a new spiritual walk.

    I. **The Conspiracy**
   II. **The Confrontation**
 III. **The Confession**
       A. A Reverence for Joseph's Position
       B. A Review of Joseph's Proposal
       C. A Restatement of the Problem
       D. A Request for Pity
  IV. **The Genuineness of Their Repentance**
   V. **The Realization of Their Self-Centeredness**
  VI. **The Response to Their Situation**

J oseph had fed his brothers, and to their great surprise, seated
them all in chronological order. The boys still don't know his
identity, but they must have known something strange was
going on. Joseph was attempting to see if their jealous hearts
had changed, if they would rejoice in a special blessing toward
Benjamin, or if they would respond the same way they did toward
Joseph twenty years earlier. So before his brothers leave the palace,
Joseph hatches a conspiracy to test them once again.

The Conspiracy

> And he commanded the steward of his house, saying,
> "Fill the men's sacks with food, as much as they can
> carry, and put each man's money in the mouth of his
> sack. Also put my cup, the silver cup, in the mouth of
> the sack of the youngest, and his grain money." So he
> did according to the word that Joseph had spoken. As
> soon as the morning dawned, the men were sent away,
> they and their donkeys (Genesis 44:1-3).

Earlier in his life, Joseph's brothers had conspired against him in
hate. Now Joseph conspires against his brothers in love. Those boys
are about to experience a plan laid out by God and executed by
Joseph for the purpose of bringing them face-to-face with their sin.

There are two things going on in Joseph's conspiracy. First, he
is testing the greed of his brothers. Instead of taking their money,
he has it stashed back in their bags, to see what they will do with
it. Remember, these are men willing to sell their own brother for
twenty shekels of silver. Finding the money in their sacks brings
back the memory of their blood money. Joseph wants to see what
impact their guilt has on their actions.

A second element of this conspiracy is that it tests their attitude.
Joseph put his silver cup into Benjamin's sack to find out if the
others see Benjamin as a threat, just as Joseph had been a threat to
them. He wanted to know what his brothers would do when they
found the cup in Benjamin's sack, sitting there like a ticking time
bomb, ready to explode at any minute.

The Confrontation

"When they had gone out of the city, and were not yet far off, Joseph said to his steward, 'Get up, follow the men; and when you overtake them, say to them, 'Why have you repaid evil for good? Is not this the one from which my lord drinks . . . ?'" (vv. 4-5). Joseph sent his servant to instigate a confrontation with his brothers, and they were offended by his remarks.

> And they said to him, "Why does my lord say these words? Far be it from us that your servants should do such a thing. Look, we brought back to you from the land of Canaan the money which we found in the mouth of our sacks. How then could we steal silver or gold from your lord's house? With whomever of your servants it is found, let him die, and we also will be my lord's slaves." And he said, "Now also let it be according to your words; he with whom it is found shall be my slave, and you shall be blameless." Then each man speedily let down his sack to the ground, and each opened his sack. So he searched. He began with the oldest and left off with the youngest; and the cup was found in Benjamin's sack (vv. 7-12).

Those boys must have felt some relief as each bag was opened and no cup came out. They were sure they had done nothing wrong. But when the very last bag was pulled open and the silver cup came sparkling into the sun, they were filled with terror. They tore their clothes, which people in Old Testament times did when scared and sorrowful, and immediately they returned to the city to face Joseph. The thought of returning to Jacob without Benjamin put them in a frenzy.

"So Judah and his brothers came to Joseph's house, and he was still there; and they fell before him on the ground. And Joseph said to them, 'What deed is this you have done?'" (vv. 14-15). Joseph is trying to find out if the brothers still had jealous hearts. Were they willing to take up the cause of an accused brother? Would they be willing to throw him away, like they did Joseph, or would they stand by him? You see, when Joseph had Benjamin served the five extra portions of food, the brothers could have masked their feelings about Benjamin. Now they could simply let Benjamin be carried off into slavery, while they returned to Canaan with the grain. Joseph had to discover whether or not his brothers had really changed.

But the Scriptures reveal right away the change that had taken place in the lives of these men. As soon as Benjamin gets in trouble, they start back to Egypt to accompany Benjamin to his trial. They go right to Joseph to protest their brother's innocence. Joseph argues with them that he can "practice divination," which in this case means that he can determine what is really going on. He can tell if a man is guilty or innocent. Joseph brought his brothers into a confrontation, and now he will discover whether or not they have truly experienced a change of heart.

The Confession

Judah, who had apparently taken his unstable brother Reuben's place as spokesman for their group, addressed Joseph to make a confession: "What shall we say to my lord? What shall we speak? Or how shall we clear ourselves? God has found out the iniquity of your servants; here we are, my lord's slaves, both we and he also with whom the cup was found" (v. 16). Joseph had been waiting for one of the boys to stand up and confess their sin. Judah was not confessing to stealing the cup; he knew none of his brothers had stolen the cup. Instead he is confessing that twenty years ago he and his brothers had committed a grievous sin. He is admitting, "God has found us out. We are guilty." They were innocent of stealing the cup, but guilty of stealing their brother's life.

What followed was a lengthy discourse by Judah to Joseph, retelling the entire story of their travels from Canaan to Egypt, Jacob's reluctance to allow Benjamin to accompany them, and his grudging acceptance of their plan. But Judah notes, "When I come to your servant my father, and the lad is not with us, since his life is bound up in the lad's life, it will happen, when he sees that the lad is not with us, that he will die" (vv. 30-31). Then Judah makes an incredible offer: "Now therefore, please let your servant remain instead of the lad as a slave to my lord, and let the lad go up with his brothers. For how shall I go up to my father if the lad is not with me, lest perhaps I see the evil that would come upon my father?" (vv. 33-34). This is an incredible offer on behalf of Judah. The former rebel, who had married a pagan and eventually committed incest, was now offering himself as a replacement for Benjamin. This intercessory work offers a picture of how we should intercede for our brothers before God, and I believe this is the reason Judah was selected to be the progenitor of Jesus Christ. There are at least four principles from Judah's prayer in verses 18-34 that we can glean.

A Reverence for Joseph's Position

"Then Judah came near to him and said: 'O my lord, please let your servant speak a word in my lord's hearing, and do not let your anger burn against your servant; for you are even like Pharaoh" (v. 18). Here Judah shows great honor and reverence for Joseph, who stands before him in the place of God. When it comes to praying, God is worthy of honor and praise. We ought to go before Him with a sense of awe and majesty. Something inside me cringes whenever I hear someone speak to God with too much familiarity, as though he can bring God down to our level. We are not to bring the Lord down, but to raise ourselves up. Judah understood that when he dealt with the most powerful person in Egypt, who held Judah's life and the lives of his brothers in his hands, the proper approach is one of reverence. Judah came to Joseph in an attitude of humility and honor to intercede for his brother, and we ought to approach God in that same way.

A Review of Joseph's Proposal

The second thing Judah did was to review Joseph's proposal. In verses 19-24, he restates everything they had been asked to do. It's as though he is saying, "Remember, you told us exactly what to do, Joseph, and we did it." Joseph had told the boys to go home, get their youngest brother, and bring him back to Egypt. The brothers had done that, though it took a long time, and they'd had to argue with their father about it. But the bottom line is that they had obeyed what Joseph had said.

If you want to add power to your intercessory prayers, get yourself into a situation where you can respond like Judah did. Make sure you can say, "Lord, all those things you told me to do, I did. I obeyed you." There is power in an obedient life. Joseph had to listen to a man who completed every task he'd been given.

A Restatement of the Problem

The third principle is the importance of restating the problem.

Judah lays out the entire story for Joseph, telling exactly what his father had said and how they had responded. In essence, Judah is explaining the exact problem. He says, "Our father's life is completely wrapped up in his youngest son's life. If we go back without the boy, our father will just die." He lays out all the details, to make sure everything is clear.

In my own life, I've found the best praying I do is when I can get someplace alone and lay it all out before the Lord. I'll just go someplace quiet, where there will be no interruptions, and pour out my heart to Him. I'll give God all the details. Sure, He already knows them, but my talking through them allows me to see them in a new light. Restating the problem is key to being effective in prayer.

A Request for Pity

Finally, in verses 32-34, Judah asks for Joseph's pity. After coming reverently before him and carefully explaining the situation, Judah gets to the heart of the matter. He explains exactly what he would like to have happen. That's important in prayer. We have to tell God what we want Him to do.

What do we want God to do? It's strange just how many of our prayers never get to the issue. We'll talk and talk, but never explain what we want Him to do for us. But Judah got to the point: "Let him go, and let me stay." It's no wonder that Joseph could restrain himself no longer. Chapter 45 reveals that, after hearing Judah's request, Joseph burst into open weeping, unable to control his emotions. But before we explore Joseph's response, consider this question: Why did Joseph wait so long to reveal himself to his brothers and forgive their sin? He knew who they were immediately, so why bother with all the testing? I can see three important reasons.

The Genuineness of Their Repentance

First, Joseph wanted to make sure his brothers had repented of their sin. He found his answer in Judah's request. Judah finally admits the sin of the boys and takes responsibility for the consequences. He shows that his heart has changed.

When we stand before the Lord, we must begin by repenting of our sin. The revelation of Christ won't come until we have repented. If we want God's majesty in our lives, the only way it will happen is to come to terms with our sin and repent of it. In waiting, Joseph gave his brothers adequate time to discern the genuineness of their repentance. Rather than putting celebrities on stage as soon as they leap from the baptismal font, as we so often do, we ought to allow time to make sure their conversion is real, not just an emotional high. Genuine repentance is critical to anyone approaching the Lord.

The Realization of Their Self-Centeredness

Joseph waited to forgive his brothers until he saw how they treated each other. When Joseph had grown up in that family, the brothers were violent, cruel, and selfish. Now they were willing to put their lives on the line for one another. Something had begun to soften their hearts, so that life was no longer bound up in selfishness. Instead, they demonstrated their love for God by their treatment of others.

I've found that nothing reveals our attitude toward God quite as much as our attitude toward other people. Show me a selfish man who doesn't care about anyone other than himself, and I'll show you someone who is not under the control of the Holy Spirit. Joseph was waiting to see whether or not his brothers had learned to care about others.

The Response to Their Situation

These men, who had walked independently of the Lord and taken on the ways of Canaan, at last had begun to see that God was involved in their lives. They had realized that they were being punished by God for their sin against Joseph. They could see that God had His hand on their lives. He was always at work, even when those brothers neglected Him. He is always at work in our lives, whether we acknowledge Him or not.

Joseph, in seeing that his brothers now understood the role God had played in their lives, was ready to reveal himself.

1. In Genesis 44, what conspiracy did Joseph start?

Why did he do that, rather than reveal himself to his brothers?

Why did Joseph select Benjamin to receive the cup?

What does Judah confess in verse 16, and what does that mean?

2. If we are to come before God with reverence, what right does God have to be revered? Base your response on the following passages:

Psalm 8:1-9

Psalm 9:1-5

Psalm 11:1-10

Psalm 19:1-11

Psalm 24:1-2

Psalm 65:1-13

Psalm 66:1-7

Psalm 93:1-5

Psalm 104:1-13

3. How can a reverent spirit affect our prayers?

What would you say to someone who said he or she prayed "to the man upstairs"?

What does reverence say about our attitude toward the Lord?

4. Why is it helpful to restate the problem when going before the Lord?

Have you ever been helped by talking through the details of a situation with the Lord? When?

Why is it a good idea to ask the Lord for something specific?

5. What does Judah ask of Joseph?

Why do you suppose that is significant?

How does Joseph's response reveal the significance of that request?

6. How would you define prayer?

Why do we pray?

How would you answer someone who claimed, "If God knows everything, we don't need to pray"?

7. As you consider the lessons of this chapter, examine your life. Is there anything about which you need to repent?

What is your attitude toward others, and how does that reflect your attitude toward the Lord?

How are you seeing God at work in your life today?

8.   Spend some time in prayer, asking the Lord to help those around you who have needs.

DID YOU KNOW?

The cup, which actually belonged to Pharaoh, was part of Egyptian culture. It would be filled with gold and precious stones, and then the Egyptians would do incantations over it in an attempt to learn the future or speak to the dead. I'm sure Joseph would have none of that, but as Pharaoh's representative he would have kept a cup like that in his house, and here he had a chance to use it to teach his brothers a lesson.

JOSEPH REVEALS HIS IDENTITY

Genesis 45:1-15

In this chapter we'll see how Joseph revealed himself to his brothers, and what lessons we can apply to our own lives.

OUTLINE

I. **The Revelation**
   A. A Private Revelation
   B. A Painful Revelation
   C. A Powerful Revelation
   D. A Passionate Revelation
II. **The Reconciliation**
III. **The Responsibility**

Twenty-two long years had passed since Joseph was separated from his family by the hostility and jealousy of his brothers. Joseph had been forced to follow a different path than that of his brothers, but eventually the two paths would merge again. In Genesis chapter 45, Joseph and his brothers are reunited, never again to be estranged. The story of their reconciliation is one of the most moving in all of Scripture. Joseph, who had tested his brothers to see if they were still the same, arranged for the youngest one, Benjamin, to be caught with Joseph's cup in his sack. When the brothers come face-to-face with Joseph and reveal their concern for Benjamin, Joseph sees that their hearts have in fact been changed.

The Revelation

Then Joseph could not restrain himself before all those who stood by him, and he cried out, "Make everyone go out from me!" So no one stood with him while Joseph made himself known to his brothers. And he wept aloud, and the Egyptians and the house of Pharaoh heard it. Then Joseph said to his brothers, "I am Joseph; does my father still live?" But his brothers could not answer him, for they were dismayed in his presence. And Joseph said to his brothers, "Please come near to me." So they came near. Then he said: "I am Joseph your brother, whom you sold into Egypt. But now, do not therefore be grieved or angry with yourselves because you sold me here; for God sent me before you to preserve life. For these two years the famine has been in the land, and there are still five years in which there will be neither plowing nor harvesting. And God sent me before you to pre- serve a posterity for you in the earth, and to save your lives by a great deliverance. So now it was not you who sent me here, but God; and He has made me a father to Pharaoh, and lord of all his house, and a ruler throughout all the land of Egypt (Genesis 45:1-8).

Joseph finally reveals himself to his brothers in a scene so sublime it barely seems real. This loving man, who has come to recognize the hand of God in his destiny, reaches out to the very brothers who thought so little of his life that they sold him into slavery. There are several things to notice about this revelation.

A Private Revelation

First, it was a private revelation. Joseph wanted the moment to be intimate, so he cleared the room of all Egyptians. The only people left were Joseph and his brothers. It was a time of intimacy between family members, so Joseph made sure no one but family was in attendance.

After all the events that led up to this encounter, you might think Joseph would have had a long and impassioned speech to give to his brothers, but he didn't. All he says is, "I am Joseph." Those words put terror into the hearts of his brothers. "I am Joseph," he says to them, and the simplicity of that revelation creates a sense of drama even today. It was a private moment, which Joseph reserved just for himself and his brothers.

A Painful Revelation

Joseph next asks, "Does my father still live?" His brothers, too terrified to even speak, didn't answer. As Joseph revealed himself, his brothers just stood and stared, wondering if it could really be their long-lost sibling. In verse 12 Joseph says, "Your eyes and the eyes of my brother Benjamin see that it is my mouth that speaks to you." In other words, Joseph was no longer pretending not to understand Hebrew. He threw out the interpreter and was speaking directly to his brothers for the first time, so when he announced, "I am Joseph," the brothers must have been completely struck dumb. They could not answer. What a painful revelation! Imagine the caution with which they must have inched toward Joseph when he called for them to get closer. But as they come in close and they see his features and the resemblance to Benjamin, they begin to recognize that this is indeed the brother they sold into slavery years earlier.

Back into their minds flood the pain and guilt of their sin. The long secret that they had covered up was now out in the open. The object of their hatred stood before them, and they were terrified in his presence. What would he do to them? How would he respond to the very men who had sold him like an animal? This was a revelation that brought pain and terror to their hearts.

A Powerful Revelation

It's strange that Joseph doesn't rebuke them. He never points his finger and says, "Now I'm going to get even!" He doesn't reprove them at all or give any cause for them to think he might be angry with them. His entire speech is couched in terms of concern for his brothers: "Do not be therefore grieved or angry with yourselves;" "God sent me;" "It was not you who sent me here, but God." After encouraging them not to feel bad, he reminds them of the sovereignty of God.

One of the greatest assets Joseph had was his sensitivity to every situation. In both his triumphs and tragedies, Joseph was able to see through his circumstances and find God at work behind the scenes. He understood the concept Paul wrote about in Romans 8:28: "All things work together for good to those who love God." Joseph always seems to be conscious of God in his life. He refused the invitation of Potiphar's wife because he recognized that it would be "a sin against God." He refused to exalt himself when interpreting Pharaoh's dream, instead insisting that "God shall give Pharaoh an answer." Now he refuses to take vengeance upon his brothers for selling him as a slave, since he now knows the Lord had it in mind all along. Joseph made God part of every aspect of his life. He understood that he wasn't just sold by his brothers, he was sent by God. He knows that the Lord wanted to use him to save lives in Egypt. Rather than being angry, Joseph is rejoicing in the Lord that he has his family back.

If we can come to a place in our spiritual walk where we can see God at work in both our triumphs and tragedies, we'll find new peace in our souls. We don't always understand or particularly like what God arranges, but we understand the fact that He is in charge, and we bow to His sovereignty. That's called living with an eternal perspective, and it's exactly what Joseph does in chapter 45. He has confidence that God is at work on His master plan, regardless of how the immediate circumstances appear. Joseph's life was a ministry, and his powerful revelation to his brothers was couched in terms of ministry.

A Passionate Revelation

This was no detached, objective revelation of himself. Verse 14 says that he "fell on his brother Benjamin's neck and wept, and Benjamin wept on his neck. Moreover, he kissed all his brothers and wept over them." Kissing was the Old Testament form of expressing affection, and Joseph kissed them all. He kissed Reuben, who was as unstable as water. He kissed Simeon and Levi, two guys who were always getting into trouble. He even kissed Judah, who first made the suggestion to sell Joseph. He wrapped his arms around his siblings and kissed them, offering the most passionate of revelations.

Joseph was a passionate man. It's amazing to see how many times he cried in Scripture. He wept in the pit, he wept when he was sold, he wept when he heard his brothers talking about their sin, he wept when he asked about Benjamin, and now he is weeping over Judah's selfless speech. Later we'll see how Joseph weeps upon seeing his father, and again at his father's funeral, weeping tears of regret that his brothers are still under a cloud of guilt for their actions. Our culture says that men cannot weep, that they need to be "macho" and not reveal emotion, but Joseph was always willing to reveal himself. It's all right to cry. The Bible even tells us that Jesus wept, and some of the most godly men I know are sensitive and can weep at something moving or touching. Joseph's revelation to his brothers moved him deeply, so he wept.

The Reconciliation

Now that Joseph was revealed, there was a reconciliation in the family. Those brothers, torn apart for twenty-two years, were welded back together by the grace of God. There would be no more holding back, no more waiting, and no more wondering about his father and brothers. Joseph was reconciled to his brothers. I can think of at least four things that come as a result of being reconciled. First, there was *peace*. Joseph was finally at peace with himself. He was at peace with his brothers. As soon as he revealed himself to his family, the result was a peace in the heart of everyone involved. Second, there was *protection*. The brothers came, fearful of Joseph and what he might do to Benjamin, but as soon as they discovered he was their brother, all fear disappeared. They felt protected, for they knew Joseph would care for them.

Third, there was a sense of *provision*. Remember, they had come to Egypt seeking something to eat, and Joseph was in charge of all the food resources in the known world. In addition, Joseph would soon send for the rest of the family and promise to give them all new things when they arrived. Joseph promised provision for his family. Finally, there was a new *proximity*. Joseph invited his brothers to come near him. He hugged them and kissed them. After all that time apart, he wanted to be close to his family. The fellowship and oneness those brothers experienced that day must have been something wonderful to behold.

The Responsibility

After Joseph revealed himself, he gave his brothers a task to accomplish:

> Hurry and go up to my father, and say to him, "Thus says your son Joseph: 'God has made me lord of all Egypt; come down to me, do not tarry. You shall dwell in the land of Goshen, and you shall be near to me, you and your children, your children's children, your flocks and your herds, and all that you have. There I will provide for you, lest you and your household, and all that you have, come to poverty; for there are still five years of famine'" (Genesis 45:9-11).

Joseph told his brothers to go get his father and to do it with haste. He invites his family to come join him in Egypt, where he has the power to take care of them. That's why this is not simply a historical picture, but a prophetic picture. We are the brothers estranged, and Jesus (like Joseph) is revealed to us when we find Him as Savior. When we first met the Lord, it was in *private*, and it was *personal*, and it might have been *painful* for us. The Bible says that the first work of the Spirit is to convict of sin, and there is usually pain associated with sin. The pain in the revelation of Joseph was wrapped up in the fact that his brothers knew they'd done something wrong. When they finally saw Joseph as the man he was, the guilt of all their sin came in upon them and filled their hearts with terror. Many people, upon meeting Christ, develop an overwhelming feeling of having offended the Lord, or of having walked in opposition to His way. It was painful to give up ourselves and commit our lives to Christ, but it was also *powerful*. Christ offered us forgiveness, just as Joseph forgave his brothers. The power of that revelation is what overwhelms us and brings us to a *passionate* faith in Christ.

When Jesus walked up to Mount Calvary and stretched Himself

out upon that cross, it was evidence of His love. It was not a detached revelation of God, but a passionate revelation of the Lord dying in our place, beckoning us to come because we now see that what He says in the Bible has been proven by His deeds. Once the Lord was revealed to me, I had *peace* in my soul. My burden was lifted; I had peace within myself for the first time ever. I felt at peace with God, and I had a wonderful sense of *protection*. I came to God with a sense of fear, but then I found protection in Him; I never have to fear the fires of hell or the wrath to come, for I have been saved from those. And if God has given me eternal life, He will also freely give all things, so I'll have no worries about *provision*. He has set a spiritual table before me, filled with the blessings of the spiritual life. And I have *proximity*, knowing the Holy Spirit lives inside my heart, and I can talk to God at any moment because we are in a relationship with one another.

Now, I've been given a *responsibility*, just like Joseph's brothers. They were asked to go tell someone, and I have been asked to go tell everyone. Jesus is alive, and part of my job is to tell others that fact. He has been exalted and sits at the right hand of God, making intercession for us and beckoning others to join Him. Joseph is a picture, a "type" of Christ. He is an Old Testament illustration of a New Testament truth.

Like Joseph's brothers, we are being called to reconcile ourselves to Him and unite with Him in order to be saved. Then it is our responsibility to be ambassadors of reconciliation everywhere, preaching the Good News of the living, exalted Jesus Christ who tells us to come unto Him.

APPLICATION

---

1. When did you first meet Jesus Christ? What were the circumstances?

What attracted you to the Lord?

Was it a painful time for you? Why or why not?

Was it an emotional time for you? In what way?

2. How did Christ bring peace to your soul?

What sort of protection do you sense from being in the Lord?

What provision do you have in Christ?

3.   If someone were to ask you why you're a Christian, what would you say?

4.   What principles for remaining close to God can you glean from the following passages?

Psalm 11:1-2

Psalm 118:1

Psalm 147:1

Psalm 150:1-6

Proverbs 1:7

Isaiah 6:1-4

Revelation 4:3-11

Revelation 15:2-4

How did Job, Abraham, and Moses remain close to God in Job 1:1-5, Genesis 12:1-9, and Deuteronomy 12:1-7?

5. Habakkuk was another character who went through hard times in order to be prepared by God. In Habakkuk 1:1-4, what is his complaint?

How does the Lord respond in verses 5-11?

How would you sum up the response of Habakkuk in 1:12—2:1?

What were the people like in Habakkuk's day?

How did Habakkuk's attitude change?

6. As you read Habakkuk chapter 2, what parallels to our culture do you see?

What does God say is going to happen to the people?

How would you describe Habakkuk's new attitude in chapter 3?

What do you think changed it?

7. Have you ever experienced a low time like Habakkuk?

What caused it?

How did you get out of it?

How does remaining close to God help us get beyond our immediate circumstances?

What are you doing right now to draw closer to the Lord?

DID YOU KNOW?

The root word for *worship* is the Greek term *gonu*, which means "to bend the knee." (We get the word *genuflect* from it.) In Old Testament times, a man or woman would bend their knees when in the presence of someone greater than themselves. Joseph had dreamed his brothers would bend their knees before him, and that's exactly what they did, admitting his superiority over themselves. The early church, recognizing this as a gesture of humility and submission, incorporated the practice of congregational kneeling in prayer early in the second century.

Lesson 5

UNDERSTANDING GOD'S BLUEPRINT

Genesis 45:16-46:27

In this chapter we will take a look at the "big picture"
of God's plan and the steps Joseph went through
to complete that plan.

OUTLINE

E veryone wants to know if God has a purpose for his life. The story of Joseph reveals not only that God has a plan for each of us, but that He is at work behind the scenes to make it happen. This chapter will focus on the blueprint God has for our lives.

   I. **The Information Step**
  II. **The Confirmation Step**
     A. People
     B. Provision
 III. **The Application Step**
 IV. **The Confrontation Step**
  V. **The Inspiration Step**
 VI. **The Realization Step**

N ow the report of it was heard in Pharaoh's house, saying, "Joseph's brothers have come." So it pleased Pharaoh and his servants well. And Pharaoh said to Joseph, "Say to your brothers, 'Do this: Load your animals and depart; go to the land of Canaan. Bring your father and your households and come to me; I will give you the best of the land of Egypt, and you will eat the fat of the land. Now you are commanded—do this: Take carts out of the land of Egypt for your little ones and your wives; bring your father and come. Also do not be concerned about your goods, for the best of all the land of Egypt is yours. . . .'" Then they went up out of Egypt, and came to the land of Canaan to Jacob their father. And they told him, saying, "Joseph is still alive, and he is governor over all the land of Egypt." And Jacob's heart stood still, because he did not believe them. But when they told him all the words which Joseph had said to them, and when he saw the carts which Joseph had sent to carry him, the spirit of Jacob their father revived. Then Israel said, "It is enough. Joseph my son is still alive. I will go and see him before I die" (Genesis 45:16-19; 25-28).

One of the most difficult questions that troubles mankind is, "What is my purpose in life?" I'm convinced that most people do not fear death near as much as they fear ending their lives without having accomplished any of the purposes they intended. What an awful thing to come to the end of one's days, only to see that God's purpose has been missed. As a pastor, I often have young people ask me about their purpose in life, their careers, schooling, and marriage decisions. There is great sincerity and urgency for those who want to know God's will, and the good news is that the Bible tells us we can know what God wants us to do. The accomplishment of God's plan is the greatest joy you'll ever experience. Those who have searched and discovered it are the ones who seem to walk closest to the Lord.

In this chapter, God's purpose for one family is made explicitly clear. As we explore the story, we'll see some excellent principles for finding God's will for our own lives. God has a blueprint, a plan for His people, and that included a plan for Jacob's little clan. Long before Joseph was born, God appeared to Abraham, his great-grandfather, and told him what would transpire. God said,

> Know certainly that your descendants will be strangers in a land that is not theirs, and will serve them, and they will afflict them four hundred years. And also the nation whom they serve I will judge; afterward they shall come out with great possessions. Now as for you, you shall go to your fathers in peace; you shall be buried at a good old age. But in the fourth generation they shall return here, for the iniquity of the Amorites is not yet complete (Genesis 15:13-16).

Abraham's great-grandchildren were going to experience something rare. They were going to be transported out of Canaan into a foreign nation to serve for 400 years, and they would end up as slaves. But after those years were up, God promised Abraham they were going to leave that foreign nation with great possessions.

In God's blueprint, part of that prediction is about to come true. God's perfect plan is going to unfold exactly the way He said it would. And just as the Lord had a plan for Jacob's family, He also has a plan for our lives. We'll never be truly happy until we find out His plan and activate it. There are several things we can learn about God's "blueprint" in the story of Joseph.

The Information Step

If God is going to get Jacob and his family from Canaan to Egypt, they'll need the right information. So when Joseph reveals himself to his brothers, he says, "Hurry and go up to my father, and say to him, 'Thus says your son Joseph: 'God has made me lord of all Egypt; come down to me, do not tarry'" (Genesis 45:9). He tells his brothers to hurry up and move the family under his protection. Joseph is God's instrument to give information concerning His plan to the people of Israel.

Before the Bible was written, God spoke through individuals to accomplish His plan. But in our time, God has a wonderful information device called Scripture, and between its covers are the principles that give us the information we need to live our lives. The Bible is God's inerrant, infallible Word, His revelation to all mankind. In the Bible you can find out what God wants you to do. "I will instruct you and teach you in the way you should go," it says in Psalm 32:8. If we have the right attitude toward God, we can come to His information book and find His purpose for our lives. The reason most people aren't sure what God wants them to do is because they don't spend any time looking in His Word for information. If we don't get into the Bible to find out what God wants us to know, we'll jump from one thing to another, never feeling confident that we're in His will. We need to assume the responsibility to dig through His Word. We need to collect all the information we can, get all the principles together, and list them alongside the things we know about ourselves and our God-given abilities. In the process of pulling all that information together, God will direct us. He always does, if we're faithful to do our part.

The Confirmation Step

The second step in discerning the plan of God is to get some confirmation. Inevitably when God tells us to do something from His Word, it will not only be impressed upon our hearts, but confirmed in our lives in a number of ways.

People

"Now the report of it was heard in Pharaoh's house, saying, 'Joseph's brothers have come.' So it pleased Pharaoh and his servants well" (Genesis 45:16). The king and his servants were in agreement that Joseph's family should join him in Egypt. It's scary when somebody we trust, someone with a heart for God, is not in harmony with what God has told us to do. In my own life, any time the Lord has spoken clearly to me through His Word, it isn't long before someone is coming alongside to say, "You know, you're doing the right thing."

There are certain kinds of people to whom we'll want to go for confirmation of God's will. Some will try to talk us out of His will, and others will try to impose their own will, but there is a certain type who will confirm God's call to us. First, the person we go to must have shown wisdom in managing his own affairs. If we've got a friend who doesn't know what he is doing, we shouldn't ask him what to do! Second, the person ought to have no ulterior motive, but genuinely care about our growth and well-being. Third, we should ask a person who is kind and reflects the attitude of Jesus Christ. A person who loves us can have the courage to be honest with us, even if he thinks we won't like what he has to say. Fourth, the person to whom we go for confirmation needs to be a positive person who believes God leads us through problems, and who is willing to help us sort through the alternatives. When we find that sort of person, we should tell him or her what we think God is calling us to do. Inevitably that individual will be God's tool to confirm our decision.

Provision

When Joseph informed his brothers that they were to bring Jacob back to Egypt, suddenly everything they needed to accomplish the journey was provided for them. Pharaoh promised them the best land and carts to haul things with, and he even promised to replace their old furniture with new stuff. Joseph provided them with provisions, new clothes, food, money, and donkeys with which to carry everything. He provided everything they would need. That sort of confirmation by provision is exactly how God lets us know that we are on the right track.

The Lord isn't going to ask us to do something impossible. If He gives us a direction, He is obligated to help provide the means to get there. It may not be the way we expect, but it will be God's way. "Those who seek the Lord shall not lack any good thing," it says in Psalm 34:10. The provision always accomplishes God's direction. He will supply the provisions we need to complete His plan.

The Application Step

The next step is often hardest of all. We can have all the right information, and have it confirmed in our minds by our friends, and even have the money in hand to do it, but if we don't obey, nothing will happen. The hardest part is taking a step in the right direction. It's wonderful to talk about moving to another country as a missionary, until the moving van picks up all the furniture and sticks it in storage. That's when we know this moving stuff is for real. That's why I appreciate verse 21 of chapter 45: "Then the sons of Israel did so." They had the information, they had people confirming it, and God had supplied them with the needed provisions, but those men had to start walking toward home if they were to really put God's plan into action. The hardest thing in the world is to start obeying.

That's been true in my life. I can know the right decision to make and be sure it's the correct move, but to actually make the change is tough. For example, the day I placed a resignation letter on a desk so that I could change jobs was one of the hardest days of my life. But that's the step of faith we must take if we want to accomplish God's purpose. We must step out in faith and apply what we know to be true.

The Confrontation Step

I've never seen things work out any other way. When we set out to do the will of God, we get the information, it's confirmed by those we believe and trust, then we take the step of faith and immediately run into some obstacles. Confrontation almost always happens. It even occurred with Joseph. He knew what to do, and Pharaoh agreed with him, and the brothers set out to apply their knowledge by bringing the entire family back to Egypt. But then they stood in front of Jacob and ran into a problem. "And they told him, saying, 'Joseph is still alive, and he is governor over all the land of Egypt.' And Jacob's heart stood still, because he did not believe them" (v. 26).

Isn't it always that way? We just get going in the right direction, when before we know it we have a confrontation with somebody who doesn't believe it. Unbelief is the greatest obstacle to the expression of faith in the life of Christians. Unbelief has ruined the vision of more people than any other single characteristic. One of the reasons so many churches settle for mediocrity is because they are limited by their unbelief.

We ought to pray every day, both corporately and as individuals, that God would never limit us through our own unbelief. We have everything we believe God can give us, so sometimes we set barriers on our lives because we won't believe great things. Matthew 13:58 tells of Jesus coming to Nazareth and not doing many miracles "because of their unbelief." On another occasion the Lord said the reason his disciples couldn't heal an epileptic man was because they didn't have enough belief that it could be accomplished. The greatest problem we face in churches and Christian colleges is the problem of unbelief. Doubt creeps into the hearts of those who should be walking in faith and trusting God for His provision.

Unbelief settles into their lives like a dark cloud, wiping out God's plan and destroying the opportunity for His miracle-making power to take place. There will always be confrontation with unbelief for anyone willing to do great things for God.

The Inspiration Step

I love the words in Genesis 45:27: "But when they told him all the words which Joseph had said to them, and when he saw the carts which Joseph had sent to carry him, the spirit of Jacob their father revived." If his heart had stopped in verse 26, it was revived in verse 27. What caused the unbelief of Jacob to turn into faith? Inspiration.

I think there are three elements to inspiration. First, there are *words*. Jacob was revived by the words he heard. His sons started telling him everything that had happened. Jacob began to listen to his boys talking about Joseph, and through the words he began to get inspired. His unbelief melted away. He developed faith. When I'm sure I'm on the right path, and suddenly run into confrontation, it is nearly always overcome through words. I get my nose into a Bible and study it, and suddenly the Lord speaks to me through a verse. Recently I was tired and cranky about something, but as I read my Bible I came across this verse: "Ah, Lord God! Behold, You have made the heavens and the earth by Your great power and outstretched arm. There is nothing too hard for you" (Jeremiah 32:17). As I thought about that verse, I got so happy and excited that my fatigue left me! My heart was revived and inspired because of those words.

A second element of inspiration is *works*. Notice that it was when Jacob "saw the carts which Joseph had sent" that his spirit got revived. It's great to get a word, but it's even better to see some hard evidence. If the words couldn't revive Jacob, the wagons could! God promises to supply all our needs, and it is inspiring to see Him work even in a small way.

The third element of inspiration is *worship*. The first part of chapter 46 tells us that

> Israel took his journey with all that he had, and came
> to Beersheba, and offered sacrifices to the God of his
> father Isaac. Then God spoke to Israel in the visions of
> the night, and said, "Jacob, Jacob!" And he said,

"Here I am." So He said, "I am God, the God of your father; do not fear to go down to Egypt, for I will make of you a great nation there. I will go down with you to Egypt, and I will also surely bring you up again; and Joseph will put his hand on your eyes" (vv. 1-4).

Jacob, an old man who had thought for years that his son was dead, is suddenly told that Joseph is alive and rules all of Egypt. He struggles in believing it, but he sees the wagons full of provisions and realizes it must be true, so he starts on his way to Egypt. He takes the step of faith and obeys God. In the midst of a worship service, God speaks to him to say, "You're on the right path, Jacob. I want your family in Egypt. Someday you'll be a great nation, and then I'll call your family back to Canaan. And Joseph, the boy you thought had died, is not only still alive, but will be at your bedside and close your eyes when you die."

Jacob's heart was renewed. It wasn't beating the same way any more; now it was pounding in excitement. He had a word from God, he had seen the works as evidence, and now his worship time had inspired him even more. God's blueprint was being followed.

The Realization Step

Then Jacob arose from Beersheba; and the sons of Israel carried their father Jacob, their little ones, and their wives, in the carts which Pharaoh had sent to carry him. So they took their livestock and their goods, which they had acquired in the land of Canaan, and went to Egypt, Jacob and all his descendants with him. His sons and his sons' sons, his daughters and his sons' daughters, and all his descendants he brought with him to Egypt (Genesis 46:5-7).

At last the plan of God was realized. His chosen people were getting out of Canaan and into a land where they could grow and be protected. Jacob's obedience allowed God to turn Israel into a great nation.

There is one interesting postscript, however. Pharaoh had said that Jacob could leave everything behind, but the text notes that Jacob's family loaded up everything and brought it with them.

They couldn't leave their junk behind. It's like when we move, and we have things we haven't touched in ten years, but instead of throwing them away we pay to have them moved with us. Jacob was just like that. He couldn't quite trust that everything was going to be as promised. Still, all of this moving was part of God's blueprint. Everybody involved had become part of the process. The Lord shared information, they got it confirmed, were willing to obey it, faced the confrontation of unbelief, but were inspired to keep going, and eventually realized the dream.

If Jacob and his family had stayed in Canaan, they would have been absorbed into the culture. The Canaanites were the most vile, pagan people who ever walked this earth. They were so bad that, 400 years later when God called Israel back to the promised land, He ordered their total annihilation. So God had Israel settle for a time in the land of Goshen, the best land in Egypt, protected and isolated. They would be under the protection of Joseph, the most powerful man in the kingdom. God knew exactly what He was doing. His plan was perfect for Joseph and his brothers, and it is perfect for us.

APPLICATION

1. In one sentence, what do you believe is your purpose in life?

Why?

What are you doing right now that will help you to achieve that purpose?

Is there anything that you need to stop doing to better achieve that purpose?

2. In your own words, what do we mean when we refer to the "will of God"?

What does Isaiah 25:1-4 say about the overall plan of God?

3. What are we promised in Isaiah 46:10-11?

What promise does the Lord make to us in Psalm 32:8?

What principle can be found in Psalm 25:12?

4.   What would you answer to a friend who asked, "How can I know the will of God for my life?"

Where do you usually get information on God's will?

With whom do you seek confirmation? Why do you choose them?

5. Give an example of how you have received confirmation from another Christian regarding some important decision.

Have you ever experienced the Lord's special provision as confirming evidence of a decision? What were the circumstances?

Why is the application step a necessary part of the process? What does that step reveal about a person?

6. Read Hebrews 3:12. Why is unbelief considered "evil" by God?

What principle do you glean from Matthew 13:58?

When have you struggled with unbelief in your own life?

7. What inspires you?

How can God use you to inspire others?

Why does worship play such a significant part in our personal inspiration?

8. In a few sentences, tell why Goshen was the ideal spot for Jacob's family.

What was God's plan for Israel?

In what areas could God be leading you?

DID YOU KNOW?

God's plan for Israel was worked out perfectly. The Lord had been concerned about His people intermarrying with the Canaanites, but in Egypt there was no such concern. The Jews came to live as shepherds in a land that despised shepherds, so there was very little chance of Jacob's family intermarrying with the Egyptians. Their occupation fit beautifully into a setting where God could isolate them for years, and they could grow into a nation without compromising their culture.

Lesson 6

JOSEPH'S FAMILY REUNION

Genesis 46:8-47 & 50:1-13

*This lesson will focus on one of the few happy
families in Scripture.*

OUTLINE

The list of names in Genesis 46 tells us much about Joseph's family, and it offers insight into what makes a healthy family operate.

   I. **Joseph's Family**
  II. **Joseph's Father**
     A. Caring for His Father
     B. Loving His Father
     C. Proud of His Father
     D. Protective of His Father
 III. **Joseph's Farewell**

T he Book of Genesis offers a sad story of family life. In the first three chapters we find the foundational statements concerning the home and family, and one would think the book would be filled with success stories of family life. But in fact the reverse is true. The Bible recounts the sordid stories of broken covenants and misused trusts. Before the Book of Genesis is over, nearly every perversion of family life is illustrated in its pages. For example, early in the book we meet Lamech, who becomes a polygamist against the instruction of God. Then there is Ham, who mocks the nakedness of his father in the ninth chapter. Abram has an adulterous affair in the sixteenth chapter, Sodom and Gomorrah are destroyed because of homosexuality in the nineteenth chapter, and Lot gets drunk and commits incest with his daughters in that same passage. Abraham tempts Abimelech to lust after Sarah in the twentieth chapter, Isaac shows preferential treatment to Esau in the twenty-fifth chapter, and in chapter thirty-eight, Judah sleeps with his daughter-in-law, Tamar. By the end of Genesis, we've pretty well seen every evil imaginable in a family. The family seems like it's falling apart right after God created it, and we are still living with those same problems in our own day. But that's why this chapter of Genesis is so exciting. The story of Joseph's family pulling together offers a glimmer of hope that families who have trouble can still work out their problems and develop the sort of atmosphere God intended.

Joseph's Family

In Genesis 46 we are told that Jacob and his family are about to move into Egypt, where they will join their long-lost brother Joseph. Two verses provide a summary of the journey: "All the persons who went with Jacob to Egypt, who came from his body, besides Jacob's sons' wives, were sixty-six persons in all. And the sons of Joseph who were born to him in Egypt were two persons. All the persons of the house of Jacob who went to Egypt were seventy" (Genesis 46:26-27). Verses 8-27 list the names of all the people who went with Jacob. We won't examine every name, but there are a few interesting observations to be made simply by looking over the list.

The list of names includes Jacob, his twelve sons, his one

daughter, fifty-two grandchildren, and four great-grandsons. Those seventy people went into Egypt, and there are a few intriguing notes about some of them. For instance, after listing the five sons of Simeon, the text adds, "and Shaul, the son of a Canaanite woman" (v. 9). So apparently Simeon had married a member of the cursed race. Unlike Judah, Simeon continued in his callous fashion as a carnal man. In contrast, verse 12 records nothing about Judah's wife being a Canaanite, for he had redeemed himself and the Lord had covered his sin. God delights in forgiving the sins we have fully confessed. He not only forgives it, He forgets it. The Lord forgot that Judah's two boys were born of a Canaanite woman.

This chapter also tells us that Benjamin had ten sons and that Dan had only one. God reminds us through this passage that He keeps track of details. Nothing is lost in His sight. He knows our families and can tell us about each person individually.

Joseph's Father

Nowhere else is there a finer revelation of Joseph's character than in his relationship with his father. His respect for Jacob is a testimony to all of us as to how we ought to treat those who grow old in our households. The way Joseph asked after his dad and the concern he showed for taking care of the old man reveal a deep respect and love.

Caring for His Father

> Then he sent Judah before him to Joseph, to point out before him the way to Goshen. And they came to the land of Goshen. So Joseph made ready his chariot and went up to Goshen to meet his father Israel; and he presented himself to him, and fell on his neck and wept on his neck a good while. And Israel said to Joseph, "Now let me die, since I have seen your face, because you are still alive" (Genesis 46:28-30).

Joseph, who as a seventeen-year-old boy was doted on by his father, found himself in a position of taking care of his father. Joseph made sure his dad's needs were met.

Erma Bombeck used to tell the story of driving her car with her aged mother by her side. As they were driving down the highway, someone pulled out in front of them, and her first reaction was to reach her hand out to keep her mother from hitting the dash-board. As soon as she did so, her mind went back to all the times her mother had done that to her as a little girl, and she realized that what everyone says is true: As you age, you reverse roles with your parents. Erma was now the mother, her mom was the little girl, and Erma was watching out for her. That's similar to the role Joseph now plays, having determined to take care of his father's needs.

Loving His Father

The reunion of father and son is one of the most emotional moments in Scripture. It is a tear-filled reunion, one of seven times Joseph is described as crying. He cries tears of joy because he is so happy to be reunited with the father he hasn't seen in more than twenty years. It wouldn't be hard to film that story and make it into a popular movie, for it is truly a moving occasion. The love Joseph and his father have for each other is demonstrated by their physical affection.

Proud of His Father

One of the best lessons in this chapter concerns Joseph's pride for his father. In a land where shepherds were despised, Joseph brings his father Jacob, the shepherd, into a face-to-face meeting with Pharaoh. There is no shame at all in Joseph. He doesn't hide his father out of embarrassment or try to deny their connection. Instead, Joseph proudly brings his father into Pharaoh's court to meet the king. Though Joseph is by now a cultured Egyptian and Jacob a peasant shepherd, Joseph introduces him to the most pow-erful man in the world with great pride.

"Joseph brought in his father Jacob and set him before Pharaoh; and Jacob blessed Pharaoh" (v. 7). Jacob, his skin weather-beaten and his clothes simple, must have seemed out of place surrounded by the flaunted finery of Pharaoh's court. As he walked slowly in front of the line of guards, limping on his bad thigh, the old man doesn't bow before the king. Instead he raises himself to his full height, draws out his gnarled, sunburned hands, and blesses Pharaoh. Hebrews 7:7 notes that "the less is blessed by the better." For you see, Jacob understood things as they really are. Although he was just a nomadic shepherd, he knew he was a child of God. As such, his possessions were of greater value than all the worldly possessions Pharaoh could name. Pharaoh might be lord and prince here on earth, but Jacob was a prince of God in heaven. I'm sure the fact that Jacob wasn't struck down on the spot is a testimony to Pharaoh's respect for Joseph.

Pharaoh then asks a rather odd question of Jacob: "How old are you?" (v. 8). The people of Egypt didn't live to be as old as the Hebrews did, so Pharaoh had probably never seen anyone as old as Joseph's father. Jacob answered by saying, "The days of the years of my pilgrimage are one hundred and thirty years; few and evil have been the days of the years of my life, and they have not attained to the days of the years of the life of my fathers in the days of their pilgrimage" (v. 9). What a sad reply! In essence, Jacob tells the king of Egypt that his life has been short and sorry. He had lived a hard life, and his sorrow was partly from his own actions and partly from spending twenty years separated from his beloved son. He had cheated some, been cheated by others, and watched his boys go astray from what he knew was right. Jacob had a tough life, but he could look back and see God's miracle-working power on his behalf.

Protective of His Father

Not only was Joseph proud of his dad, he was protective as well. Joseph did at least three things to keep his father safe and secure. First, he gave him *position*. He located Jacob in Goshen, an area east of the Nile River that was fairly isolated. It was an extremely fertile place with great pastureland for their sheep and was the part of Egypt nearest to Canaan, so it would make for an easy exodus 400 years later. When Joseph offered Goshen to his family, it made for an ideal position to grow the family and yet to keep the family together.

A second thing Joseph did was give Jacob *possessions*. Verse 11 states that "Joseph situated his father and his brothers, and gave them a possession in the land of Egypt, in the best of the land, in the land of Rameses, as Pharaoh had commanded." Jacob's family now had possession of the perfect piece of property on which to shepherd.

Third, Joseph gave him *provisions*. "Then Joseph provided his father, his brothers, and all his father's household with bread, according to the number in their families" (v. 12). He took care of everyone's needs, acting almost as a father would to a son. Joseph arranged for a place near to himself, met every need, and gave his father all the provisions he would need in the years ahead.

Joseph's Farewell

Though he was old, Jacob lived for seventeen more years in Goshen, under the protection of his son, Joseph.

> So Israel dwelt in the land of Egypt, in the country of Goshen; and they had possessions there and grew and multiplied exceedingly. And Jacob lived in the land of Egypt seventeen years. So the length of Jacob's life was one hundred and forty-seven years. When the time drew near that Israel must die, he called his son Joseph and said to him, "Now if I have found favor in your sight, please put your hand under my thigh, and deal kindly and truly with me. Please do not bury me in Egypt, but let me lie with my fathers; you shall carry me out of Egypt and bury me in their burial place." And he said, "I will do as you have said." Then he said, "Swear to me." And he swore to him. So Israel bowed himself on the head of the bed (Genesis 47:27-31).

Jacob's last request was that he not be buried in Egypt. He even had Joseph swear to it, using an old Hebrew custom of placing one's hand under the thigh. In Genesis 49:29 we read that Jacob wanted to be buried "with my fathers in the cave that is in the field of Ephron the Hittite." Here is a beat-up old shepherd who has been living in Egypt for seventeen years, and on his deathbed he wants it known that he is not to be buried in Egypt. The later chapters explain how Joseph told Pharaoh, who gave his permission to take Jacob's body to Canaan and bury it. As a matter of fact, the king gave Jacob a royal funeral, complete with dignitaries and all the important people in Egypt. If we had been living in Canaan at that time and had seen the long funeral train come over a hill, we would have assumed an important Egyptian had died. For Pharaoh was honoring Jacob because of his son Joseph. The king loved and respected Joseph so much he was willing to grant a royal funeral to Joseph's father. What a wonderful picture of respect and dignity!

Joseph would one day ask for the same thing: to be buried in

Canaan. He didn't want his bones in Egypt but in the promised land. That is a great testimony of faith. As a matter of fact, when the writer to the Hebrews crafted the "hall of fame" in Hebrews chapter 11, the notation he makes about Joseph is not overcoming temptation or enduring through hard times, but that "Joseph, when he was dying, made mention of the departure of the children of Israel, and gave instructions concerning his bones" (Hebrews 11:22). Joseph knew that what God had promised, He would deliver. The Lord had said to Abraham that the people of Israel would sojourn in a foreign land, be afflicted for 400 years, but then move back into the promised land. So when Joseph asked not to be left in Egypt, he was saying that he believed in God's promise. God said it would happen, so even though it was hundreds of years in the future, Joseph wanted to make sure he was part of the celebration.

There are at least three lessons we can learn from the story of Joseph and his family. First, God provided for the entire family due to the faithfulness of one member. God provided good land, met their every need, and watched Jacob's family come back to Him, and none of it would have happened had it not been for Joseph. Jacob was a deceiver, Reuben was unstable, Simeon and Levi were killers, and Judah was an adulterer. All of them had turned away from the Lord. But out of that family there was one who remained faithful to God. And through his faithfulness, Joseph's entire family was redeemed. Christians, if we are the only godly people in our families, we can't quit. We have the potential of redeeming our entire family.

A second lesson we learn from this story is that we are to care for the elderly. Joseph sets an example for us to follow by offering tender, loving care to his father. We need to provide for our parents and make sure their needs are met.

Finally, we learn that God puts a priority on the family. There may be many examples of dysfunctional families in Scripture, but here we have an example of a healthy, redemptive family. They went through some stormy weather, but they made it. The family is part of God's perfect plan for the world. There are only two institutions that God ordained: the church and the family. In this day, when families are being torn apart, the story of Joseph is a clear indication of what the family can accomplish when it is intact and focused on the Lord.

APPLICATION

1. In your view, why did God ordain the family as the essential building block of society?

What is the purpose of the family?

What are the elements in our culture that are destroying families?

2. How did Joseph care for his father?

What is our culture's view of the aged, and how does it differ with the biblical perspective?

What promise is associated with Exodus 20:12?

What does it mean to "honor" your father and mother?

3.   What principles for families do you find in the following passages from Proverbs?

Proverbs 1:8-9

Proverbs 10:1

Proverbs 13:1

Proverbs 13:24

Proverbs 15:12-20

Proverbs 18:22

Proverbs 19:13-14

Proverbs 22:6

4.   What is God's principle for marriage in Genesis 2:24?

How would you describe the act of "leaving" in that verse?

What does it mean to be "joined together"?

5. Read Proverbs 31:10-31 and make a list of the characteristics of the virtuous wife.

What impact does she have on her children?

How does she influence her husband?

How does this description relate to our modern world?

6. In Ephesians 5:22-6:4, how is the father in the home depicted?

What does he do to build the family?

What is his goal, according to this passage?

7. In 1 Peter 3:1-6, what instruction is offered to wives?

Using this passage, what advice would you give to a woman married to a non-Christian?

What attitude is the husband supposed to manifest in verse 7?

What principles for healthy families do you find in verses 8-9?

DID YOU KNOW?

The meaning of the name *Goshen* is "to draw near." The land where Joseph's family settled was a place where he could draw near to his brothers, where his family could draw near to each other, and where everyone could draw near to God. Before, they had been scattered and feared being assimilated into the Canaanites. Now they could draw near and be isolated from the other tribes. It was in Goshen that the nation of Israel really "drew near" to one another.

JOSEPH AND CRISIS MANAGEMENT

Genesis 47:13-26

This chapter will examine how Joseph handled an emergency situation in Egypt.

OUTLINE

T he story of Joseph is one long study of crisis management. First he had to deal with personal crises, like the death of his mother and the jealousy of his brothers. Then he had to deal with the crises of other people, like the life-threatening famine that swept over the land. Genesis 47 describes how Joseph managed to successfully work through a potentially devastating crisis.

   I. **The Control of the Purses of the People**
  II. **The Control of the Possessions of the People**
 III. **The Control of the Property of the People**
  IV. **The Control of the Positions of the People**
   V. **The Control of the Production of the People**
  VI. **Principles for Crisis Management**

J oseph had a major problem on his hands. After seven years of abundant harvests, there came seven years of famine. It was Joseph's job to see the country through that difficult time. Of course, he knew it was coming, since he had interpreted Pharaoh's dream and explained exactly what the problem would be. But that didn't make it any easier on those who were starving. Genesis 41:54-56 records that

> the seven years of famine began to come, as Joseph had said. The famine was in all lands, but in all the land of Egypt there was bread. So when all the land of Egypt was famished, the people cried to Pharaoh for bread. Then Pharaoh said to all the Egyptians, "Go to Joseph; whatever he says to you, do." The famine was over all the face of the earth, and Joseph opened all the storehouses and sold to the Egyptians. And the famine became severe in the land of Egypt.

The next few chapters detail how Joseph became reconciled to his family, but at the same time he was administrating a government that was facing a national crisis.

In Genesis 47:13, the focus returns to Joseph and how he dealt with that crisis. The famine had grown to full height, and the Egyptians realized that there was no hope apart from Joseph. They were willing to submit to him at all costs and on any terms. Egypt was bankrupt and its condition hopeless, so Joseph offered the best solution. He brought everything under the authority of the throne as the only safeguard for the future. Joseph became the savior of the world in the physical realm, just as Jesus is the Savior in the spiritual realm. And Joseph's solution of bringing everything under the king's throne to save the people is parallel to Christ's solution. The Lord Jesus brings all those who are willing under His throne of grace, and they are saved for all eternity.

The Control of the Purses of the People

Joseph begins to move everything under the authority of the king. First he took control of the purses.

> Now there was no bread in all the land; for the famine
> was very severe, so that the land of Egypt and the land
> of Canaan languished because of the famine. And
> Joseph gathered up all the money that was found in
> the land of Egypt and in the land of Canaan, for the
> grain which they bought; and Joseph brought the
> money into Pharaoh's house (Genesis 47:13-14).

People could no longer trust in money, because they no longer
had any. They had used every last cent to buy bread. So Joseph
collected all that money and put it under the authority of Pharaoh.
All men, rich and poor, were reduced to the same level. The econ-
omy was in Pharaoh's hands. The purses of the people were under
the control of the throne.

The Control of the Possessions of the People

> So when the money failed in the land of Egypt and in
> the land of Canaan, all the Egyptians came to Joseph
> and said, "Give us bread, for why should we die in
> your presence? For the money has failed." Then
> Joseph said, "Give your livestock, and I will give you
> bread for your livestock, if the money is gone." So
> they brought their livestock to Joseph, and Joseph
> gave them bread in exchange for the horses, the flocks,
> the cattle of the herds, and for the donkeys. Thus he
> fed them with bread in exchange for all their livestock
> that year (vv. 15-17).

The very wealthy might have been able to hold out a bit longer,
but eventually everyone gave in. The power of the throne was
advanced for the good of all. The throne was in control not only
of their purses but of their possessions.

The Control of the Property of the People

> When that year had ended, they came to him the next
> year and said to him, "We will not hide from my lord
> that our money is gone; my lord also has our herds of
> livestock. There is nothing left in the sight of my lord
> but our bodies and our lands. Why should we die
> before your eyes, both we and our land? Buy us and our

land for bread, and we and our land will be servants of
Pharaoh; give us seed, that we may live and not die, that
the land may not be desolate." Then Joseph bought all
the land of Egypt for Pharaoh; for every man of the
Egyptians sold his field, because the famine was severe
upon them. So the land became Pharaoh's (vv. 18-20).

All of the fixed and liquid assets were in the hands of Joseph.
He had taken control of their purses, their possessions, and their
property.

The Egyptians were brought to the end of themselves. Their
total and unquestioning trust was placed in Joseph. Wanting to
end divided loyalties and human rivalries, Joseph created a benefi-
cent, efficient, centralized rule. Little by little he brought everything under the control of one crown.

The Control of the Positions of the People

"And as for the people, he moved them into the cities, from one
end of the borders of Egypt to the other end" (v. 21). Joseph
began to redistribute the population of Egypt, setting them up in
cities near the food supplies. A concentration of power in the
throne was taking place, so Joseph exercised his right to redistribute the population so that the manpower and resources could be
best utilized.

The Control of the Production
of the People

Then Joseph said to the people, "Indeed I have
bought you and your land this day for Pharaoh. Look,
here is seed for you, and you shall sow the land. And it
shall come to pass in the harvest that you shall give
one-fifth to Pharaoh. Four-fifths shall be your own, as
seed for the field and for your food, for those of your
households and as food for your little ones." So they
said, "You have saved our lives; let us find favor in the
sight of my lord, and we will be Pharaoh's servants."
And Joseph made it a law over the land of Egypt to
this day, that Pharaoh should have one-fifth, except for
the land of the priests only, which did not become
Pharaoh's (vv. 23-26).

Joseph took the production of the people and concentrated it, making it a means of blessing to all the land rather than a means of oppression. The resources could now be managed for the good of all. He had earlier used this same "twenty percent principle" to save for the years of famine, and now he makes that tax a permanent institution in order to finance a centralized administration.

Joseph was under no obligation to do any of this for the people of Egypt. He set up a system that treated everyone equally. Some have criticized Joseph for taking advantage of the people's difficulty and usurping all power, but if we read the story carefully we see that's not what happened at all. The people were about to lose everything. There was no food and no hope for survival. So Joseph took charge of all the resources, reorganized them, and returned them back to the people with the charge to be stewards over them. He only required a twenty percent return for the good of all Egypt. If you aren't sure of his motives, consider the response of the people. Rather than being angry or bitter, they came to him with gratitude for developing a fair plan that protected lives. Saved and sustained by Joseph, they willingly gave back their twenty percent.

Principles for Crisis Management

As I read through this chapter, I find Joseph exemplifying some abiding principles that I can adopt. First, I am reminded that crises are no respecter of *persons*. They come to all of us at one time or another. Nobody can expect to elude crises forever. Even the wealthy and the elevated of Joseph's time were brought low by this crisis.

Second, I see that crises cause us to re-examine our *purpose* in life. How Joseph managed things is a real encouragement to me, because it causes me to think through what God wants to do in my life. Pharaoh had told the people exactly what to do in their crisis: obey Joseph. And God has told us exactly what to do in our crises: obey the Word. Pharaoh told the people to listen to Joseph, and God has told us to listen to Jesus. In the midst of crises, we often have to stop and ask ourselves, "What are we doing? What does God want us to do? Am I being responsible and obedient to Him?" Sometimes we just need to re-examine our purpose and make sure we are fulfilling God's desire for our lives.

Joseph became the savior of Egypt. Everyone turned to him and became loyal to him. When things are going well it's easy to say the words, "Whatever you say, I'll do." But in the midst of a crisis, we have to stop and ask some basic questions to make sure we're doing the right things. Nobody wants to go through a crisis and then say, "I wish I'd done something else," and nobody wants to come to the end of his life and say, "I wish I'd done something else with my life." Crises help us to focus on what's really important. They help us re-examine our purpose in life.

A third principle I get from this story is that crises cause us to re-evaluate our *priorities*. The people of Egypt were like people everywhere: concerned about making money, gaining more things, and moving up in society. But when the crisis came, none of those things mattered. They gave away their land, they gave away their money, they gave away their cattle—they even gave away themselves in order to survive. What would cause anyone to do that? Because above all they wanted to survive. Gold and status mean nothing to a starving man. When a crisis hits, we focus on the things that really matter. Usually we'll find that the crisis isn't really life-threatening anyway. When we go through tough times, we'll find ourselves thinking about what's really important to us.

Fourth, crises cause us to re-establish our *principles* in life. We find out what we really believe when we're faced with utter turmoil. For example, notice that Joseph took all the land except for that which belonged to the priests. He was unwilling to take over the sacred things, for they were more important than the immediate troubles. When we run into a crisis, we should ask ourselves what is really sacred. What would we be unwilling to give up? Chances are we'll find out that a few things are sacred, but nothing is secular. Some things are untouchable, but God is involved in all of it. Whatever we do is all to His glory.

Nothing was secular to Joseph. He did everything to honor God. In times of plenty, he lived for the Lord, and in times of crisis, he lived for the Lord. Joseph understood that all of life is part of God's plan, even the crises. As a matter of fact, the crises reveal to us how strong we really are. If our lives are built firmly on our faith in God, we can stand firm in the midst of disaster. But if our lives are built on unstable principles of man, any disaster will bring us to ruin. As I look at Joseph's life, I'm reminded that this godly man never got free from trouble. And if he didn't, why should I expect to? I'm going to face hard times in my life, but the good news is that I can stand as God's man in the face of those troubles, for my life is built on Him.

1. What steps did Joseph take to get control of Egypt?

Why was it important for him to do so?

What was the result of his actions?

How did the people respond?

2. How would you reply to someone who said, "Joseph manipulated everyone! He took advantage of their situation to build up the government?"

What in the story points to Joseph's integrity throughout this crisis?

Why do you think integrity is essential to make Joseph's plan work? What would happen to that plan if the leadership had no integrity?

What management principles can you glean from Joseph's handling of the famine?

3. What crises have you faced in your life?

Are you satisfied with how you handled each crisis?

How did they cause you to re-examine your purpose in life?

What is your purpose in life?

What lessons or principles did you learn?

4. What would you say are your top three priorities?

How well does your schedule reflect your priorities?

How well does your checkbook reflect your priorities?

If someone could follow you around and observe your life for one week, what would they say were your top priorities?

5. Read Matthew 7:24-27. What is the meaning of Christ's parable?

In practical terms, who is the fool and who is the wise?

How can people build their lives upon the rock of Jesus Christ?

6.   Take a few moments to reflect on the purpose and priorities of your life. What are your goals? What do you hope to accomplish for the Lord? Make a list of the things you want to be, the things you want to do, the things you want to have, and the people you want to help in this world.

DID YOU KNOW?

J oseph helped to set up one of the benevolent monarchies of history. The Second Intermediate Kingdom of Egypt, or Hyksos period, was perhaps the height of Egypt's power. Pharaoh retained all power, but the populace lived in a largely class-free society. As other Pharaohs abused that power, the empire went into decline. Eventually Joseph's reforms were dropped entirely. Exodus 1:8 tells us that "a new king over Egypt, who did not know Joseph," came to power, indicating a new dynasty.

JACOB'S FINAL THOUGHTS

Genesis 48:1-22

In this chapter we'll examine the events surrounding the death of Jacob.

OUTLINE

I t's hard to talk about death, but we know it is something each of us will face. The death of Jacob offers us some direction regarding how to prepare for death and how to pass the years of life.

   I. **Jacob Looked Backward in Gratitude**
      A. He Remembers Bethel
      B. He Remembers Rachel
      C. He Remembers the Angel
  II. **Jacob Looked Upward in Faith**
III. **Jacob Looked Outward in Love**
IV. **Jacob Looked Forward in Hope**

I n many ways, the Book of Genesis is a graveyard. It contains the story of how death started. Right near the start there is the death of Abel, then eventually there are the deaths of everyone during the flood, and throughout the text we are confronted with the deaths of individuals. The fifth chapter tells us, "So all the days of Seth were nine hundred and twelve years; and he died . . . So all the days of Enosh were nine hundred and five years; and he died . . . So all the days of Cainan were nine hundred ten years; and he died." It's not very encouraging reading! Death is inevitable, so it shouldn't surprise us that the last few chapters deal with the deaths of Jacob and Joseph.

I believe the death of Jacob gives us some direction as to how we can best prepare for our own deaths. I also believe the words of Jacob on his deathbed can help us know how to live our lives, knowing death is coming. Jacob is a study in contrast; the first part of his life is wild and unruly, the second part settled and godly. All the things God did in between are interesting to us, for they seem similar to the things we often find happening in our own lives. As I've observed the events surrounding Jacob's death, I find four directions that occupy his attention.

Jacob Looked Backward in Gratitude

"Now it came to pass after these things that Joseph was told, 'Indeed your father is sick'; and he took with him his two sons, Manasseh and Ephraim. And Jacob was told, 'Look, your son Joseph is coming to you'; and Israel strengthened himself and sat up on the bed" (Genesis 48:1-2). Jacob felt better, now that his favorite son was visiting him. He sat up and began to talk of all the highlights of his life.

In his closing days, Jacob wanted to look back over the events that had befallen him. As we get older, we begin to reminisce. I've listened to my grandparents tell the same stories again and again, enjoying the opportunity to look backward in gratitude to the Lord for His many blessings. They love to tell those stories to friends and family, remembering the many good things of life. As we listen to Jacob, it's interesting to see the things that occupy his attention as he takes a broad glance back through his life.

He Remembers Bethel

Joseph and his two sons are standing before Jacob. And Jacob says, "God Almighty appeared to me at Luz in the land of Canaan and blessed me, and said to me, 'Behold, I will make you fruitful and multiply you, and I will make of you a multitude of people, and give this land to your descendants after you as an everlasting possession'" (vv. 3-4). First, Jacob remembers Bethel, a place which had great meaning for him. It was in Bethel that Jacob twice met God and received a special promise. The first time was when he was running away from the wrath of his brother Esau, who was mad at having been cheated out of his blessing. Jacob stopped at Bethel, and it was there God appeared to Jacob and said He had a special plan for his life. Jacob was afraid and burdened down with guilt when God took the opportunity to minister to him.

On another occasion, recorded in Genesis 35, the Lord appeared to Jacob at Bethel and spoke with him. That's when God changed his name to Israel and promised to make him into a great nation. God took a special interest in Jacob's personal needs at Bethel, so Jacob remembers the spot with fondness.

He Remembers Rachel

"But as for me," Jacob says to Joseph, "when I came from Padan, Rachel died beside me in the land of Canaan on the way, when there was but a little distance to go to Ephrath; and I buried her there on the way to Ephrath (that is, Bethlehem)" (v. 7). Jacob had several wives and had sons by two of their handmaids, but there was always only one person in his life who had real meaning to him: Rachel. Jacob is 147 years old in this chapter, and his wife had died more than two decades earlier, but he never forgot her. She was still the most important memory in his life. As he reviews the high points of his existence, the one thing he can't forget is the woman he loved with all his heart. I'm sure that as Joseph, Rachel's son, and Ephraim and Manasseh, Rachel's grandchildren, stood before Jacob, it caused him to think back to the joy he had known with her. He had worked fourteen long years to win her hand, only to lose her in death prematurely.

He Remembers the Angel

"The Angel who has redeemed me from all evil," Jacob says, his hands on his grandchildren, "Bless the lads" (v. 16). The "Angel" he refers to is an Old Testament reference to the Lord Jesus Christ. Jacob is referring to the night he wrestled with the Angel and would not quit until the Angel blessed him. Up until that point in his life, Jacob had been "the trickster." But after that experience, he became Israel—"the prince of God."

As Jacob reviewed his life, he wanted his son to understand that his life had been rich and full and that he was grateful for Bethel and Rachel and the Angel. He looked backward in gratitude, and I know that if we live our lives right and honor God, there will be much to be thankful for as we grow older. Life is never going to be one long parade of happy experiences, but with the Lord we can look back in gratitude for what He has done in our lives.

Jacob Looked Upward in Faith

Jacob knew the reality of God's presence and promises. His entire speech is punctuated with references to God's intervention in his life. That's why he starts out saying, "God Almighty appeared to me" (v. 3), continues by uttering, "God has also shown me your offspring" (v. 11), and concludes by exclaiming, "God will be with you" (v. 21). Jacob had become a God-centered person in his old age. He had been a self-centered man in his earlier years, scheming to get the things he wanted. But in his golden years something happened to make him turn his attention toward the Lord.

Jacob remembered his religious heritage. He talked to Joseph about "God, before whom my fathers Abraham and Isaac walked" (v. 15a). The Lord had walked with his father and grandfather, and now He is walking with Jacob. He also refers to "the God who has fed me all my life long to this day" (v. 15b). He'd experienced all kinds of trouble and his life was checkered with disappointment, but at 147 he could look back and see the hand of God. Even through the disappointments of Reuben and Simeon and Levi, even through the cheatings of Laban and the loss of his son Joseph for twenty years, Jacob could now see how God was walking with him all the time.

When we are passing through the trials and difficulties of life, it's not always easy for us to see the hand of God. But as we review the past and evaluate what the Lord has done, we can obtain an absolute assurance that He was with us all the way. When a Christian walks with God, he or she can look back on life and say, "Jesus was there, leading me all the way."

Jacob Looked Outward in Love

As Jacob thought of his own past and reflected upon his renewed trust in God, he could look out from his deathbed and see standing in front of him Ephraim and Manasseh. "Who are these?" he asks Joseph, his eyes almost gone. "These are my two boys," Joseph replies, and Jacob immediately wants to bless them. In the Hebrew tradition you bless the older son first, placing your right hand upon his head, then you bless the younger with your left hand. Joseph, trying to make sure they get in the right order, moved the boys closer to his father. But as he moves them close, Jacob does something surprising. He places his right hand on the younger boy, Ephraim, and his left hand on the older boy, Manasseh. Joseph tried to straighten things out, "but his father refused and said, 'I know, my son, I know. He also shall become a people, and he also shall be great; but truly his younger brother shall be greater than he, and his descendants shall become a multitude of nations" (v. 19).

God's blessing normally flowed to the oldest son, but at times He chose, in His sovereignty, to bypass the natural lines and reach out to bless another. So if we were to explore the history of Israel we'd find that Ephraim was indeed the blessed of the tribes. In fact, so blessed was this tribe that when the northern part of the kingdom split away from the southern part, it took the name of Ephraim to stand for the whole area. The two most populous tribes in Israel were the tribes of Ephraim and Manasseh. The amazing thing is that they were not, in the true sense, legitimate heirs. They were, after all, the sons of Joseph, not Jacob. And they were the sons of an Egyptian woman, not pure Jews. But God decided to bless those boys, and He did! We can't always figure out a formula for why God blesses one over another, and we'd go crazy trying to create one. We simply rejoice in the fact that God blesses us, and we ought to get on our knees and thank Him because we don't deserve it. If we don't think we're blessed as much as we should be, we ought not to complain. Who gets the blessing isn't our department, but God's. Ours is to praise Him. God blessed the sons of Joseph through Jacob, who looked outward in love.

Jacob Looked Forward in Hope

Jacob was ready to die, but he hadn't stopped believing in the future. He told Joseph, "Behold, I am dying, but God will be with you and bring you back to the land of your fathers" (v. 21). He retained a vision for his family that reached beyond the day of his own death. He trusted in God for a future blessing, knowing that his descendants would not stay forever in Egypt. Someday they would return to Canaan, and the Lord would give it to them. Jacob remembered God's promise to bless the nation with land. That's why he asked to be buried in the cave of Machpelah, where Abraham and Isaac were buried. He was a man of faith, and he knew that one day his family would return to live there.

When we look back at our lives one day, we will stand in the place of Jacob and thank God for what He has done. Christians, we can look upward with absolute confidence because God has been our Shepherd every step of the way. Then we can look forward in hope, believing God for our future.

I find three pragmatic lessons in this closing chapter of Jacob's life. First, Jacob teaches us the *purpose of passing years*. Don't allow the "youth cult" of our culture to trap you into thinking that growing old is something negative. God has a purpose in our aging. It weans us from self-worship and causes us to mature in love. Growing old is intended to make us more gentle, more thoughtful, more sympathetic, and less childish. The Lord allows trials and tribulations to make us better people. The pain, conflicts, setbacks, and disappointments we suffer are intended to help shape us into the kind of people God wants us to be. Difficulties will either make us bitter or make us better. We can view them as stumbling blocks or stepping stones to a more godly character. That's the purpose of passing years.

Another lesson we learn from Jacob's life is the *possibility of painful experiences*. Jacob's life was one painful experience after another. Most of the problems of his early life he brought on himself were used by the Lord to teach Jacob a lesson and bring him to Himself. As I've gone through hard times, I've come to realize that God wants to shape me. I haven't been shaped much by the happy experiences, but I've learned a great deal from the painful experiences. God uses them to get my attention and change me. I don't like those times, but I see them as necessary if I'm to grow up in Him.

Finally, Jacob's life teaches me the *priority of a spiritual perspective*. As he got older, he could see the hand of God at work in his life. Jacob was transformed by his face-to-face encounter with the

Lord. He was never the same after wrestling with God, either physically or spiritually. As he aged, he was able to look at all the events of his life from a spiritual perspective. As I age, I want to do the same. I want to keep a perspective of always looking to the Lord and His purpose, so that I'll remain focused on Him.

APPLICATION

1. As you read through Genesis 48, what would you say is the overall theme?

What are the key words or phrases?

What was foremost on Jacob's mind as he spoke with his son and grandsons?

2. For what did he look backward in gratitude?

As you reflect on your life, what have been the high points?

What were the low points?

How have you seen the hand of God at those times?

3. In what ways did Jacob look upward in faith?

What words express his faith?

For what do you want to praise the Lord?

4. Who is the most positive, faith-filled person you know?

What makes that person that way?

What would you say to a Christian who complained, "I just don't sense God is working in my life"?

5. What hope was Jacob looking forward to?

What hope are you looking forward to?

What do the following verses teach us about hope?

Psalm 42:5-11

Psalm 62:5-10

Psalm 71:5-18

Psalm 119:49-56

Psalm 130:1-8

Psalm 146:1-6

6. How do you think Joseph responded to his father's words?

What insights does this passage give you regarding growing older?

If you could see yourself thirty years from now, what words would you want to be used to describe you? What character qualities do you want to exhibit?

What would you need to do to develop those?

DID YOU KNOW?

The "twelve tribes" of Israel are not all named after Jacob's twelve sons. The name of Dan was dropped, due to sin, and replaced by the name of Joseph's oldest son Manasseh.

Lesson 9

A PROPHETIC LEGACY

Genesis 49:1-33

Jacob's last will and testament is the focus of this chapter.

OUTLINE

Although skeptics reject the notion of prophecy, God revealed future events through His chosen messenger at the appropriate time. Each of the prophecies Jacob made about his sons occurred, and two of them in particular offer a lesson for our times.

   I. The Fact of Prophecy
  II. The Prophecy for Reuben
 III. The Prophecy for Judah

W hen we last met with the family of Jacob, Jacob had sat up in his bed long enough to bless Joseph and his two sons, Ephraim and Manasseh. Jacob is now 147 years old, and he knows his time on earth is about over, so he brings together his twelve sons to give them his last will and testament. As he gathers them around him, he offers a blessing to each one and a prophecy concerning their future. The prophecies in Genesis 49 are uncannily accurate, and some include words of doom for his disobedient sons. As we explore them, we have the opportunity to look backward through history, to see not only the prophecies but how they were fulfilled in the tribes of Israel.

So accurate are the words of this chapter that it has become a battleground with critics of the Word of God. They can't understand how these words could be written ahead of time, so they attempt to turn Genesis 49 into a historical section, with an author putting words in Jacob's mouth describing events that had already occurred. But that's not true; this passage of Scripture literally spells out the history of the Jewish people before it happened. It takes faith to believe in prophecy, but all the evidence surrounding this chapter supports these as the words of Jacob, and we have a God we know can reveal the future through His chosen messenger.

The Fact of Prophecy

Consider one example of the accuracy of Jacob's prophecy. In verses 5-8, he prophesies concerning the tribes of Simeon and Levi, speaking of their cruelty and anger. In the seventh verse Jacob uses these words: "Cursed be their anger, for it is fierce; and their wrath, for it is cruel! I will divide them in Jacob and scatter them in Israel." Simeon and Levi were the sons who went up against Shechem and slew a whole nation because of the sin that was committed against their sister, Dinah. Jacob was angry with them because of their treachery, so he made the pronouncement that their two families would be divided.

What happened to those two tribes later was amazing. The tribe of Simeon had no inheritance when the promised land was divided. The tribe itself was scattered. They were counted along with the people of Ephraim and Manasseh and Naphtali, rather than separately. At the end of the second census, the tribe of

Simeon had shrunk and become the smallest tribe in all Israel. When Moses blessed the nation, he didn't even mention Simeon. Jacob had said the tribe would be scattered, and they did exactly that, nearly disappearing as an entity.

A different end awaited Levi. That tribe took a stand for God in a place called Baelpeor, when Israel sinned with the daughters of Moab. When Moses raised his standard and asked, "Who is on the Lord's side?", it was the tribe of Levi that responded. Because of that, the Lord turned the curse of Jacob into a blessing. The prophecy came true, but in a very different way.

The tribe of Levi was scattered throughout the land but as the priests of Israel. There were 48 cities up and down Israel that took care of the tribes of Levi. They had no inheritance, no land, and were scattered around all the other tribes. Jacob's prophecy was literally fulfilled, but it's interesting to note that the tribe of Levi became a blessing to the rest of the nation, rather than a curse.

The fact is, Jacob offered a prophecy regarding every single tribe, and every one came true. Prophecy is a fact, and Jacob gave uncanny prophecies that impacted each of his sons and the tribes which sprang from them. Two of the prophecies in particular present a powerful message to our modern world. They stand in contrast with one another, but they each have a lesson for us.

The Prophecy for Reuben

"Reuben, you are my firstborn, my might and the beginning of my strength, the excellency of dignity and the excellency of power. Unstable as water, you shall not excel, because you went up to your father's bed; then you defiled it—he went up to my couch" (Genesis 49:3-4). Jacob spoke first to his eldest son, Reuben. The name means, "Behold, a son!" and speaks of the excitement of the first child. Consider the unique situation Reuben was in: He was the firstborn son of Jacob; he stood in the place of greatest opportunity; he should have had the birthright; and his father spoke of him having the "excellency of dignity, might, and power." In other words, Reuben held the royal place of a firstborn son. It should have been a wonderful opportunity for Reuben to excel in serving the Lord. But he forfeited the privilege of the firstborn through the unconfessed sin of his life.

Reuben lost his birthright because he became sexually involved with one of his father's mistresses. He committed adultery and tried to cover it up, and that sin had apparently never been discussed between father and son for forty years. Now on his death bed, Jacob looks into his eldest son's eyes and says, "You sinned and I know it." There had been plenty of time to repent—Reuben was with his father for twenty years in Canaan and seventeen years in Egypt—but he had never done so. He had tried to cover up his sin, but at the father's final judgment seat it was exposed, and Reuben's hopes were broken.

Jacob's prophecy concerning Reuben was that, due to his unconfessed sin, his character and his future would be affected. He would always be as "unstable as water," which is to say, he would never have a strong character. His unconfessed sin gave him an unstable life.

Do you remember when you were growing up and you did something you knew was wrong? You didn't want to confess to anyone, though you felt that eventually someone would find out, so you walked around on eggs, not knowing who knew and who didn't know. You were always unsure who to talk with honestly, or what to say. There was no honesty or integrity in your life; you were as unstable as water. The result of unconfessed sin is always instability, not only spiritually but emotionally. That's exactly what had taken place in Reuben's life. And because of that instability, he would never excel. The tribe of Reuben never rose to prominence in Israel. None of his tribe ever ruled the nation. None of the judges were ever Reubenites. In fact, the tribe of Reuben was the first tribe to demand its inheritance, and the most careless of the consequences. They rashly chose the wrong side of the Jordan River to settle, rather than waiting for the best land. They were barred from the priesthood, and when you read about the terrible rebellion of Korah, the tribe of Reuben was at the forefront. When Jacob prophesied that the tribe of Reuben would never excel, he was telling the exact truth, and that truth was evidenced throughout the history of Reuben's tribe.

The Prophecy for Judah

Judah was the son who married a pagan woman and eventually slept with his own daughter-in-law. His first difficulty came when he became friendly with the Canaanites and began to interact with the evil people of his culture. Before he went down that road very far, he married a wicked woman, a woman who denied God. To their union were born three sons: Er, Onan, and Shelah. Er married a woman named Tamar, but the Bible notes that Er was so wicked that God killed him. That left Tamar a widow without children, so by custom she was given to the second son, Onan, who also did wicked things and was killed by God. Then Judah promised his youngest son to Tamar, but he didn't deliver on his promise, so Tamar tricked him into sleeping with her by dressing as a prostitute. When she became pregnant, she revealed to Judah that he was the father, and Judah confessed his sin.

Judah led a pretty rough life. But somewhere along the line something happened, because as the brothers stood before Joseph in terror during the famine, it was Judah who became the spokesman for the family. The former adulterer stepped forward and gave one of the most blessed speeches in Scripture, repenting of his sin and making things right with the Lord. Rather than trying to cover his sin, Judah brought it out into the open. For that honesty, God began to bless his life.

As we read Jacob's prophecy for Judah, it's interesting to see the notable absence of prophetic words. There is no reference to Judah's sin with Tamar, because Judah had already confessed the sin and been forgiven. So instead of talking about past mistakes, Jacob takes the time to describe the new character of the man:

> Judah, you are he whom your brothers shall praise;
> your hand shall be on the neck of your enemies; your
> father's children shall bow down before you. Judah is
> a lion's whelp; from the prey, my son, you have gone
> up. He bows down, he lies down as a lion; and as a
> lion, who shall rouse him? The scepter shall not depart
> from Judah, nor a lawgiver from between his feet,
> until Shiloh comes; and to Him shall be the obedience
> of the people. Binding his donkey to the vine, and his
> donkey's colt to the choice vine, he washed his gar-
> ments in wine, and his clothes in the blood of grapes.
> His eyes are darker than wine, and his teeth whiter
> than milk (vv. 8-12).

Reuben had been disinherited, and Judah became the primary leader in the family. Judah's tribe became the head of all the tribes of Israel. They were victorious over all of them as well, which is why "lion" is such an apt picture of their tribe. The king of the forest is a beautiful picture to describe the kingship of Judah over all other tribes in Israel. Out of Judah came the man after God's own heart, David, who is also called a "lion." And eventually there came the Messiah, Jesus Christ, who is called in Revelation the "lion of the tribe of Judah."

Judah was the largest of all the tribes throughout Israel's history and when the nation marched through the wilderness, it was the tribe of Judah that marched first, in the place of honor. Judah was the first tribe to be assigned a territory of inheritance in the land, and the first judge in the land was Othniel from the tribe of Judah. Every single king who sat on the throne from David to the captivity was from Judah's tribe, and the Bible says that in Judah we have a clear presentation of the Messiah who was to come. We can look all through the pages of Genesis and we'll never see the term *Shiloh* used again. It's the Hebrew word for "peace," and it refers to the coming of Jesus Christ. Jacob is prophesying that out of the tribe of Judah shall come the Messiah.

The sin of Judah certainly complicated his life and also the lives of his children. His deliberate sin was far greater than Reuben's, who fell into sin in a moment of passion. But Judah was forgiven because of his willingness to repent, and Reuben was forgotten. The story of Judah is a picture of our relationship with God. Judah confessed his sin, and the Lord forgave him. "If we confess our sins, He is faithful and just to forgive us our sins and to cleanse us from all unrighteousness" (1 John 1:9).

The one who tries to cover his sins shall never prosper, but the one who confesses his sins shall be forgiven. Reuben forsook the mercy of God, while Judah found His mercy. As Solomon said, "He who covers his sins will not prosper, but whoever confesses and forsakes them will have mercy" (Proverbs 28:13).

When I was a boy, I worked at a place where I could get the autograph of some pretty famous Christians, and they would always put a favorite Scripture reference under their name. One time a man signed his name and wrote underneath it, "1 Corinthians 11:31." I didn't know what that verse was, so that night I flipped to it and read the words, "For if we would judge ourselves, we would not be judged." If we take note of the sin in our lives and take the initiative to put it behind us, then the Bible says we won't be judged for that sin. But then the converse thought occurred to me: If there is unconfessed sin in our lives, and we refuse to deal with it, God will have to judge that sin. His judgment process can include sickness, pain, discouragement, financial hardship, or any number of troubling prospects, but we can count on the fact that if we don't judge our own sin, God will. Reuben tried to hide his sin for years, and it helped destroy his character and his life. On Jacob's deathbed (Jacob's judgment seat), Reuben's sin was exposed and his hopes broken. But Judah confessed and repented of his sin, and the Lord forgave him and gave him a wonderful ministry and heritage.

None of us can make it through this life without sinning. The road of life is rough, and there are ruts and potholes in which we can fall. But the Bible tells us how to deal with the sin in life: repent and confess it. If we do, God will bless. If we don't, God will judge. The choice is ours.

APPLICATION

1. What prophecy does Jacob make about Reuben in Genesis 49:3-4?

How was that accurate?

What is the result of unconfessed sin?

2. How do you define sin?

What do the following passages teach us about sin:

Psalm 32:1-5

Psalm 119:11

Romans 2:12

Romans 6:1-14

2 Corinthians 5:16-21

Hebrews 9:26-28

Hebrews 12:1-3

James 1:13-15

1 John 1:5-2:2

3. Read Psalm 51. What is the attitude of David in this psalm?

For what does he ask?

What has been the result of his sin?

What does he look forward to with forgiveness?

4. In your own words, what illustration does Paul make in Romans 7:1-6?

What is Paul struggling with in verses 7-12?

Restate Paul's main points in verses 13-23.

What conclusion does he draw in verses 24-25?

5. What practical advice does Solomon offer regarding sin in the following passages?

Proverbs 5:22-23

Proverbs 10:19

Proverbs 14:9

Proverbs 16:6

Proverbs 17:19

Proverbs 20:9

6.   What prophecy did Jacob make for Simeon and Levi in Genesis 49:5-7?

What were his words for Zebulun in verse 13 and Issachar in 14-15?

What was said of the other boys in verses 16-21 and verse 27?

What prophecy does he make regarding Joseph in verses 22-26?

7. In your own words, what is the difference between Reuben and Judah?

What principle should we take from that?

Spend some time in prayer, examining your own life in regard to
that principle.

DID YOU KNOW?

Jacob said that Zebulun would dwell by the sea, and the tribe
did, becoming rich through seaborne trade. Issachar is called a
"strong donkey," and that tribe was forced to work for the
others. The tribe of Dan was supposed to become judges and
provide justice, but as prophesied, they chose treachery and were
the first to abandon God for idols. Jacob said that Gad would be
trampled upon, and as a border tribe they were the most fre-
quently attacked. Asher became farmers, providing rich food, and
Naphtali became a mountain people, free as the deer. Joseph's
leadership fulfilled his prophecy, and the tribe of Benjamin were
violent warriors, like the wolves Jacob used to describe them.

Lesson 10

GOD MEANT IT FOR GOOD

Genesis 50:14-21

This last chapter will take a look at Joseph's humble and loving response to his brothers.

OUTLINE

Joseph had every right to be mad at his brothers, and nobody would have blamed him had he taken a measure of revenge. The fact that he didn't tells us something about his character and offers an example of how we are to cope with hurt.

   I. **A Realistic Appraisal of Sin**
  II. **A Realistic Appreciation of the Sovereignty of God**
 III. **A Refusal to Replace God in Their Lives**
 IV. **A Realistic Application of Human Sensitivity**

We all become harried, and when it gets to the point where we just can't take it any more, it's like the valve pops open. We march across the street, or into the boss's office, or over to the church, and we just let it all out. The vengeance flows. But as good as that might feel at the moment, it probably isn't right. Joseph's life is perhaps the antithesis to that sort of activity, for if there were ever a man who had reason to take revenge, it was Joseph. His family had badly mistreated him for a dream that turned out to be precisely correct. Their actions had led to years of slavery, unjust accusations, and the hardships of prison. He had every "right" to get back at his brothers . . . but he didn't.

In Genesis 50 things have changed dramatically for Joseph. His father has died, and his brothers now fear that Joseph will be looking to take revenge upon them. They believe the only reason Joseph forgave them was for their father's sake, so with their father out of the picture, there is no longer anyone to protect them from Joseph's wrath.

> When Joseph's brothers saw that their father was dead, they said, "Perhaps Joseph will hate us, and may actually repay us for all the evil which we did to him." So they sent messengers to Joseph, saying, "Before your father died he commanded, saying, 'Thus you shall say to Joseph: "I beg you, please forgive the trespass of your brothers and their sin; for they did evil to you."' Now, please, forgive the trespass of the servants of the God of your father." And Joseph wept when they spoke to him (Genesis 50:15-17).

The brothers actually sent a servant to see Joseph, with some sort of made-up statement from their father. I've searched the Scriptures and can't find any record of Jacob ever saying anything like their quotation. I think they simply felt they'd be better off if they began their argument with the weight of their father on their side: "Dad says you're supposed to forgive us."

It's not hard to understand Joseph's tears. He didn't weep because of their sin, but because the forgiveness he had already extended to them had not been accepted. Joseph was broken-hearted because he had fully forgiven his brothers, but forgiveness is never any better than our ability to receive it. The brothers had not received the forgiveness he had extended. Joseph's reply to his brothers is a model to help us know how to deal with forgiveness in our own lives and how to resist the urge to go after those who hurt us.

A Realistic Appraisal of Sin

"Then his brothers also went and fell down before his face, and they said, 'Behold, we are your servants.' Joseph said to them, 'Do not be afraid, for am I in the place of God? But as for you, you meant evil against me; but God meant it for good" (vv. 18-19). This is no cheap forgiveness Joseph offers. If he had been more like many of us, he might just have said, "Aw, forget it. It was nothing." But Joseph didn't want to underplay the actual sin. He understood that the theology of forgiveness demands a realistic appraisal of the sin which has been committed. True forgiveness can never be offered until there is an acknowledgment that a trespass has been committed. Cheap forgiveness is no forgiveness at all.

Someone has written that "Apologies keep life oiled when the bearings begin to wear," and "Nicely timed and sincerely meant, the graceful apology is a curtesy to civility." Apologies are nice, but they cannot do the job of repentance. You see, it's easy to be flippant about forgiveness. Sneaky people can use an apology as an end run. They are sorry for getting caught, and they offer a nicely phrased apology, but there is no repentance for the wrong. We've all done it at times, by saying things like, "Oh, well, I don't think it's such a big deal, but if you insist, I apologize." We want to offer some simple words to keep from dealing honestly with a complex issue. But a deep hurt isn't merely an accident; it's a sin. And sin requires confession and repentance.

I read a book recently in which the author described the four levels of repentance. The first level is the *level of perception*, in which we realize we've done something wrong. The second level is the *level of feeling*, wherein we feel the pain we have inflicted. The third is the *level of confession*, when we admit we realize we've done something wrong. The last is the *level of promise*, where we genuinely commit to not repeating our wrong action again. We've all known people who offer cheap apologies, who don't really understand or care about the hurt they've caused, and who have every intention of acting the same way again. But when Joseph was confronted by his brothers, and they admitted their sin, note that he never minimizes their actions. He says, "Yes, what you did was wrong." He recognizes the sin for what it is, so that the brothers understand his hurt.

A Realistic Appreciation of the Sovereignty of God

But notice that Joseph moves past the appraisal of sin and reveals an understanding that God is in control of all things: "But as for you, you meant evil against me; but God meant it for good, in order to bring it about as it is this day, to save many people alive" (v. 20). Joseph offers a realistic appreciation of the sovereignty of God. His brothers intended evil, but God intended good.

It's hard to put those two things together. A man can do a terrible evil toward his brother and do it with the full intention of harming him, but God can still use that sin in a positive way. Joseph is flipping their actions over to reveal God's working through the ways of men. What they meant to do is really not the most important thing. God took their evil and turned it around, making something good come from it. It takes a mighty God to be able to accomplish something like that!

The Book of James tells us that God is not tempted by evil, nor does He tempt any man. God is not the author of evil. He has no part in any evil that is done. His holy character is not reflected in sin. But sin, having been committed, is not done outside His watchful eye. Even those things which are heinous He can take and weave into the pattern of His divine purpose. In the process, God can take something that from a human perspective seems totally evil and ugly, and He can somehow work it into the beautiful tapestry of His will. Joseph understood that God is sovereign, so nothing happens to us without Him knowing it. He is in control, even when things seem completely messed up. Sometimes we want to look at the Lord and ask, "Why?" But we'd do better to take out our Bibles and ask, "Lord, how does all this fit into your plan?"

I've noticed, as I've studied the life of Joseph, that God is just as intimate to him as breath. God is so much a part of Joseph's life that he sees the Lord in every circumstance, and he trusts the Lord through every difficulty. "God meant it for good," he tells his brothers, "in order to bring it about as it is this day, to save many people alive." Everything that happened to him, both bad and good, was viewed through the lens of God's will. When Joseph interpreted Pharaoh's dream, he said that it was God who gave him the meaning. When Joseph presented his sons to Jacob, he introduced them by saying, "These are the two sons God has given me." Even when Joseph was dying, he was able to encourage those around him that "God will surely visit you." At the center of Joseph's life was the sovereignty of God. Everything that happened was for His purposes and part of His program. Even the darkest threads in the weave help to provide the overall beauty of the tapestry.

A Refusal to Replace God in Their Lives

"Am I in the place of God?" Joseph asked his brothers. He had the opportunity to take vengeance, but he refused to take God's part. If punishment was to be meted out, it would have to come from an all-wise and just God, not from Joseph. The Bible tells us that vengeance belongs to the Lord, not to us. Joseph was not willing to step into God's role. He wasn't going to use his brothers' guilt to manipulate or intimidate them.

I've known people who have gotten themselves into vengeful situations. They suffered for years by the actions of others, and now they're in a position to get even. One man was plagued by a bad boss for years, with nothing but insidious requests and unnecessary requirements. But a new company president was installed, and that man was suddenly promoted over his old boss. Now he had the opportunity to get even—or to find out if he had the character to be like Joseph.

You see, Joseph had his brothers right where he wanted them. Family influence was gone, and Joseph was the most powerful man in the world, apart from Pharaoh. But he refused to replace God in their lives. He recognized the role God plays, and Joseph refused to try and take on that part for himself. Earlier Joseph had said to his brothers,

> Do not therefore be grieved or angry with yourselves because you sold me here; for God sent me before you to preserve life. . . . God sent me before you to preserve a posterity for you in the earth, and to save your

lives by a great deliverance. So now it was not you who sent me here, but God; and He has made me a father to Pharaoh, and lord of all his house, and a ruler throughout all the land of Egypt (Genesis 45:5, 7-8).

Joseph knew that his brothers had done evil, but he also knew that God had turned that evil around for good. As he looked back over his life, he could now see the purpose behind the pain. The Lord's purpose was to save the nation of Israel, and He had accomplished it through all the events of Joseph's life.

A Realistic Application of Human Sensitivity

There is one more lesson that I get from Joseph's story, and that is the human sensitivity Joseph displays, which should always be present in the forgiver. As we look over his encounter with his brothers, we see that Joseph weeps at their request. His heart is broken for them. In verse 19 he speaks to them with words of tender endearment, encouraging them not to be afraid. And in verse 21 he encourages his brothers and tries to comfort them. There is a spirit of forgiveness in Joseph evidenced by his tender heart. It's easy to use words of apology or forgiveness but much tougher to forgive with actions of love, sensitivity, and tenderness. I cannot help but wonder if Joseph's forgiving spirit was the end product of a heart that had been broken over all the troubles of his life.

Forgiveness involves a realistic appraisal of sin, a realistic appreciation of God's sovereignty, a refusal to replace God in the lives of others, and a realistic application of human sensitivity. The sweetness and sensitivity of Joseph set an example for all of us to follow.

1. Have you ever been mistreated or shunned by someone in a way that hurt you deeply? What were the circumstances?

In your mind, how did you see yourself taking revenge on that person?

What would revenge have accomplished?

In your own words, how do you think the Lord Jesus would have you respond to that person?

2. How did Joseph first respond when confronted by his brothers in Genesis 50:15-21?

Why did he weep?

What words would you use to describe his attitude toward his brothers?

3. Why is a realistic appraisal of the sin necessary for forgiveness?

What happens if the sin is not realistically appraised?

As you look at the four levels of forgiveness, reflect on your own life. Is there anyone to whom you must go and make amends?

4. Why is it important to maintain a realistic appreciation of God's sovereignty when dealing with an issue of forgiveness? What does the sovereignty of God have to do with your situation?

As you look at the hard times you have gone through, what was God attempting to do in your life?

How could you know the Lord was behind it, using the circumstances to shape you?

5. What would you say to a person who grumbled, "Now I'm in a position to get even with that guy"?

Why does vengeance belong to the Lord?

How are we usurping God's place if we decide to wreak vengeance on someone?

6. As you look through Genesis 50, how does the sensitivity of Joseph manifest itself?

What practical steps can a person who has been hurt take to develop the feeling of forgiveness?

7. What has been your highlight in this study of the life of Joseph?

Why was that important to you?

Name three things you are going to implement in your life as a result of this study.

DID YOU KNOW?

Bible historians believe that Joseph was born to Jacob and Rachel in the year 1914 B.C., at the start of Egypt's greatest dynasties.

Turning Point
Resource Books

By Dr. David Jeremiah

Gifts from God

In the pages of *Gifts from God*, Dr. David Jeremiah comes alongside parents to say, "Be encouraged." When it's so easy for parents to be overwhelmed by the responsibilities and challenges of parenting, this book reminds us that we can raise godly children. Through personal and biblical examples, Dr. Jeremiah explains the scriptural model for turning your home into a household of faith. This book will help you realize that children are gifts from God—straight from His heart to yours.

GFGHBK (Hard Cover Book) $19
GFGSG (Study Guide) $9

God in You

Many Christians find the Holy Spirit the hardest person of the Holy Trinity to understand. Leaving abstract concepts behind, this book reveals God's Spirit in concrete terms. It brings a fresh, clear image of how the Holy Spirit affects our everyday lives as God is in us and with us.

GIYHBK (Hard Cover Book) $19
GIYSG 1, 2 (Study Guide, 2 volumes) $18

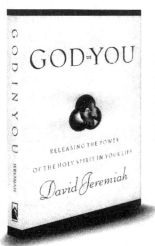

Prayer—The Great Adventure

Dr. David Jeremiah explores "The Lord's Prayer," which Jesus gave to His disciples, and explains how you can put that pattern into practice in your own life. As you study this prayer and begin to implement our Lord's teaching, you'll become more thankful for what He has done and begin to see His power at work.

PGAHBK (Hard Cover Book) $19
PGASG (Study Guide) $9

Turning Point
Resource Books

By Dr. David Jeremiah

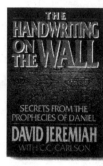
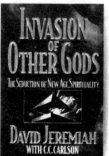
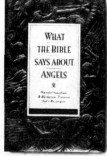

OTHER STUDY GUIDES & BOOKS AVAILABLE THROUGH TURNING POINT

Audiocassette albums are also available. For information use our toll-free number.

SELECTION	CODE	QTY	PRICE	TOTAL
STUDY GUIDES				
20:20 Network Leader's Guide	20:20G	___	$ 9	$ ___
Escape the Coming Night (Revelation, 4 volumes)	REVSG1,2,3,4	___	$ 28	___
The Power of Encouragement	POESG	___	$ 9	___
For Such a Time as This—The Book of Esther	ESTSG	___	$ 9	___
Ten Burning Questions from Psalms	TBQSG	___	$ 9	___
Knowing the God You Worship	KGWSG	___	$ 9	___
Seeking Wisdom—Finding Gold	WISSG	___	$ 9	___
The Handwriting on the Wall (Daniel, 3 volumes)	HOWSG1,2,3	___	$ 22	___
Invasion of Other Gods (New Age)	IOGSG	___	$ 9	___
Worship	WORSG	___	$ 9	___
Turning Toward Integrity (James)	TTIBK	___	$ 10	___
Turning Toward Joy (Philippians)	TTJBK	___	$ 10	___
The Power of Love (1 Corinthians 13)	POLSG	___	$ 9	___
Spiritual Warfare (Ephesians 6)	SPWSG	___	$ 9	___
Home Improvement	HMISG	___	$ 9	___
What the Bible Says About Angels	ANGSG	___	$ 9	___
Greatest Stories Ever Told (Parables)	GSTSG	___	$ 9	___
A Nation in Crisis (Joshua, 2 volumes)	NICSG1,2	___	$ 18	___
When Wisdom Turns to Foolishness (Solomon)	WTFSG	___	$ 9	___
Signs of the Second Coming (Matthew 24–25)	SSCSG	___	$ 9	___
Core Values of the Church (1 Corinthians, 3 volumes)	CVCSG1,2,3	___	$ 22	___
How to Be Happy According to Jesus (Beatitudes)	HTHSG	___	$ 9	___
God Meant It for Good (Life of Joseph, 2 volumes)	JOSSG1,2	___	$ 18	___
Christ's Death and Resurrection	CDRSG	___	$ 9	___
Prayer—The Great Adventure	PGASG	___	$ 9	___
The Life of David: The Tender Warrior (2 volumes)	TTWSG1,2	___	$ 18	___
How to Live According to Jesus (2 volumes)	HTLSG1,2	___	$ 18	___
The Runaway Prophet—Jonah	TRPSG	___	$ 9	___
God in You (Holy Spirit, 2 volumes)	GIYSG1, 2	___	$ 18	___
Ruth, Romance & Redemption	RRRSG	___	$ 9	___
Gifts from God	GFGSG	___	$ 9	___
Jesus' Final Warning (Prophecy)	JFWSG	___	$ 9	___
Giving to God	GTGSG	___	$ 9	___
Investing for Eternity	IFESG	___	$ 9	___
Living by Faith (Romans, 2 volumes)	ROMSG	___	$ 18	___
BOOKS				
The Handwriting on the Wall (Daniel)	HOWBK	___	$ 12	___
Escape the Coming Night (Revelation)	REVBK	___	$ 13	___
The Power of Encouragement	POEBK	___	$ 13	___
Overcoming Loneliness	OCLBK	___	$ 10	___
Invasion of Other Gods (New Age)	IOGBK	___	$ 13	___
What the Bible Says About Angels	ANGHBK	___	$ 19	___
Prayer—The Great Adventure	PGAHBK	___	$ 19	___
God in You (The Holy Spirit)	GIYHBK	___	$ 19	___
Gifts from God (Parenting)	GFGHBK	___	$ 19	___
Jesus' Final Warning (Prophecy)	JFWHBK	___	$ 19	___

For information and Discover, Visa, or MasterCard orders, call:

1-800-947-1993

POSTAGE AND HANDLING CHART

For Orders	Add
Up to $5.99	$1.50
$6.00-$19.99	$2.50
$20.00-$50.99	$3.50
$51.00-$99.99	$6.00
$100.00 & over	$9.00

MERCHANDISE TOTAL	___
SHIPPING/HANDLING	___
SUBTOTAL	___
CA RESIDENTS ONLY ADD 7.25% TAX	___
GIFT TO MINISTRY	___
TOTAL	$ ___

Please enclose payment with order. Make check or money order payable to:
TURNING POINT • P.O. Box 3838 • San Diego, CA 92163-1838 *(Please allow 4-6 weeks for delivery.)*

Mr./Mrs./Miss _____

Address _____

City/State/Zip _____

I listen to *Turning Point* on (station call letters): _____ Phone _____

NOTES